A Look at the
Head and the Fifty

This is the School of To-morrow: already my haunts deny me:
  I am shut out of the garden, the dusty high-road waits;
Yet ever again I turn as the milestone years flash by me
  For a look at the Head and the Fifty, and the School behind her gates;
For the hopes of youth are flowers of the field cut down, but the field
    remaineth –
        Greeting Tonbridge, Tonbridge!
        Farewell, Mother of sons!

First verse of 'Hail and Farewell', School Song, 1921.
Words by Clemence Dane, music by Dr Thomas Wood

A Look at the Head and the Fifty

A HISTORY OF TONBRIDGE SCHOOL

Barry Orchard

JAMES X JAMES

To Derek
(1924–1955)
(P. H. and J. H. 1938–1942)

ACKNOWLEDGEMENTS

I wish to thank all who have helped me in the preparation of this book, especially my three research assistants: Sally Hedley-Jones, Andrew Edwards and Andrew Zaltzman; those masters and ex-masters who have checked my preliminary efforts: Geoff Allibone, Mike Bushby, Alfred Foster, David Kemp and Jonathan Smith. I also wish to thank Jean Cook, the School Librarian for her help, and Bill Werren and Paul Thompson for their advice.

I would like to pay special tribute to Gilbert Hoole, who taught me School Certificate Latin 45 years ago and without whose knowledge of the school over a 70-year period this book would not have been possible.

I am grateful to the Governors for backing this book and to Myles Glover, the Clerk to the Skinners' Company, for sharing his knowledge with me.

I wish to acknowledge my indebtedness to previous books about the School by S. Rivington, W. G. Hart, D. C. Somervell, H. S. Vere Hodge and Gilbert Hoole.

Finally I wish to thank Stephen Campbell, the Tonbridge and Malling District Council and the New Curiosity Shop for allowing me to view and publish copies of some of the pictures and photographs in their possession.

Barry Orchard

Half-title illustration *Tennis on the Head, early 1890s*

Title page illustration *'View from the Head' (John Western)*

CONTENTS

FOREWORD

by Colin Cowdrey

Tonbridge has indeed been fortunate in her historians. Septimus Rivington produced no fewer than four editions of his scholarly work between 1869 and 1925, and, shortly after the last war, in 1947, David Somervell gave us a lively and more up-to-date version in his own inimitable style. He relied heavily on *The Tonbridgian*, the researches of the lawyer and antiquarian W. G. Hart and his own experience as a distinguished historian.

Now we have from the pen of Barry Orchard, after a great deal of meticulous research, another look at the history of the school up to 1947 as well as a perceptive assessment of the last forty years, which many of us have observed with affectionate interest, but without his intimate knowledge. As a former Head of School and long-serving Housemaster, he has played a wide variety of roles at Tonbridge. He therefore occupies an unrivalled vantage-point from which to observe the School, to comment on the stewardship of the headmasters he has known and to portray the recent developments at the School to which he has devoted most of his life. For many years he amused and delighted Old Tonbridgians with his lively annual newsletters, full of dry humour, describing everyday life at Tonbridge. This work is inevitably more measured and judicious, but no less fascinating, and it has the added advantage of some splendid photographs.

I am very happy indeed to commend this book to all fellow Old Tonbridgians, and others, who share our love for the School.

July 1991

1

THE FOUNDER

The Weald of Kent is a woody pit,
And Tonbridge lies in the heart of it:
The Medway wanders slowly down
Through fields of hop to the ancient town . . .
There lies the School!

*The Coat of Arms of the
Skinners' Company.*

Written about 70 years ago, the words above are the opening verse of one of the school songs which meant so much in those days. Now, in 1990, the Weald of Kent is less woody, the town and school have grown, the hops have come and gone, but not all that much else has changed. Looking out to the west over the Medway valley towards Penshurst on a beautiful day, it is not difficult to think back to the same scene 500 years ago when this story starts.

In 1490 England was recovering from the Wars of the Roses, and most Englishmen were thankful that the days of violence were over and they could bring up their families in peace.

There had been a crossing over the Medway at Tonbridge, probably since Roman times, and, where there was a crossing, it was almost inevitable that someone would build a fort to defend it. The Castle which dominated the town for several centuries was built just after the Norman Conquest for Richard FitzGilbert, a relative of William I, on the site of an earlier fort. No one knows when the first bridge was built, but by Norman times it had become vital to defend this important crossing on the main road from Rye to London.

There has been much argument between experts over the derivation of the name Tonbridge, and in earlier times there were many spellings – from Tunbrygge to Tonbridge. For some centuries the town was spelt Tunbridge, but, as its offspring, Tunbridge Wells, grew in size and importance, the local council decided in 1870 to adopt the modern spelling, though retaining the old pronunciation.

In 1490 the town was already quite well established and at one time in the fifteenth century sent two members to Parliament. It was also the largest parish in Kent. It consisted mainly of two groups of houses, clustered along the High Street to the north of the bridge, one group under the walls of the Castle, the other with their backs to the parish church. The town was surrounded by a fosse, traces of which can still be seen. By 1490 it had already started to extend beyond the perimeter of the Fosse, and there was a settlement on Dry Hill. To the north the road led to London, to the south to Rye. Just outside the town to the south lay a small priory and further to the west, near the river, Barden House. Round the town were several estates, all part of the extensive lands of the Lords of Tonbridge. Some of these are still there: Cage and Postern were enclosed hunting-parks; North Frith was a forest. Further to the west and north lay the estates of Penshurst, Hever and Knole.

The owner of Knole was the Archbishop of Canterbury, Cardinal Bourchier, and he employed a 'park-keeper', John Judde, who lived at Barden. Being park-keeper to the Cardinal was an honourable position, and John Judde was a gentleman and man of substance whose name is included in a list of the 'Gentils of Kent' in the reign of Henry VII. John had married Margaret Chiche, a member of a wealthy Canterbury family, and she may have been related to Archbishop Chichele, of another famous Kent family, regarded as one of the best archbishops and founder of All Souls College, Oxford. Judde was often spelt Judd in old documents, and this has also led to much argument. Vere Hodge, in his book *Sir Andrew Judde*, opted for the longer spelling and for the sake of simplicity that spelling will be used in this book.

John Judde had three sons and two daughters, and it is his youngest son, Andrew, who concerns us here. The date of his birth is unknown, but he is named in the will of his father, dated 1492, and it is probable that he was born between 1490 and 1492. His father left each of his sons property in the Tonbridge area, but he left the bulk of it to his eldest son Thomas.

Andrew grew up at Barden, and probably enjoyed a comfortable childhood, riding, hunting and farming the family land which stretched from the Medway up to Bidborough Ridge and beyond to Rusthall and Speldhurst. It is likely that he was educated at home, but if he received any extra education, it can only have been at the small priory, where boys may have been taught Latin and singing so that they could take part in the services.

When he was about 17, Andrew followed his brother John to London to make his fortune. Thomas had already gone to Oxford University to become a Fellow of All Souls, and his younger brothers had to choose

The Old Priory (drawn here by Geo. E. Mackley) whose threatened dissolution is the start of this story, fell into decay after the dissolution of the monasteries, and the remains were finally pulled down to make way for the goods yard of the railway. The present Priory Road was built over the site.

between government service and commerce. John managed to combine both careers, but Andrew seems to have decided on commerce from the outset. In 1509, according to the Skinners' Company records, he was apprenticed to John Buknell, a Skinner and Merchant of the Staple of Calais, 'to lerne the Crafte that the same John Buknell useth and to dwell wt hym . . . unto the end and terme of viii yeres'.

The livery companies of Tudor England had become more powerful over the previous hundred years and played an important role in the increasing prosperity of London as a trading centre. Since the twelfth century, traders had formed guilds both to protect their own interests and control the market in their goods. By 1509, London already controlled about 85 per cent of the trade with foreign markets, mainly those in France, the Lowlands, Spain and Portugal. By then, the London guilds had, with the help of royal charters, become more formalized and consequently more restrictive. The Skinners' Company, had, like many other London companies, evolved from a combination of a mediaeval trading fraternity and a religious guild, and its three royal charters, of 1327, 1392 and 1437 successively, confirmed its powers to control the fur trade of the whole of England.

Fur had been worn in this country at least since the days of Caesar who reported that the Ancient Britons dressed in skins. In mediaeval times it became a much-desired commodity. Furs of various types were worn both outside garments for warmth and show, and inside as lining. The variety of furs was enormous and the rules about the making and trading of fur garments extremely complex, for example, old furs must not be traded as new ones, so many furs must be used in each cloak, etc. The wearing of ermine was allowed only to royalty and nobility, though the Skinners were specially privileged to display it on their coat of arms. In addition, the making and selling of furs involved several dependent trades like the tanners and curriers.

With the other guilds controlling their trades with equally complex rules, there were naturally frequent disputes between the various companies. As the guilds developed and became more wealthy, so their position in the pecking order in London became more crucial. Disputes over precedence led to violence and even death in the streets, and the Skinners were involved in a dispute with the Fishmongers which resulted in one Skinner being hanged for murder, and in another dispute with the Merchant Taylors, which led to the famous Billesdon award in 1484. As both companies claimed the precedence of sixth position in the Lord Mayor's procession, Mayor Billesdon decreed that they should alternate on a yearly basis and entertain each other to dinner every year, which they have done ever since. This is said to be the origin of the expression 'all at sixes and sevens'.

The Staplers of Calais were not one of the City Livery guilds. Their business was the export of materials for manufacture, especially wool, hides, lead, tin and leather. Apprenticeship to them was for nine years, not eight, and freedom of the Staple gave no right to the freedom of the City of London, without which no man could trade in London. The only Staple port in 1500 was Calais, which was regarded as part of England and returned its own MPs to Westminster. It was governed by a Lord Deputy, and its mercantile community was headed by the Mayor, who in official banquets in England was placed just below the Master of the Rolls and other Justices of the Exchequer.

The beginning of the sixteenth century was also a time of voyages of discovery. The establishment of the Spanish and Portuguese empires, the voyages of Columbus, Vasco da Gama and the Cabots had excited a Europe, only just emerging from the impact of the Renaissance, the invention of printing and the recent attack on long-established religious beliefs.

London in 1509 was an exciting place to live. There was an able and attractive young king on the throne, who had not developed the despotic tendencies which were to mar his later years. Trade was flourishing, and ships were entering the docks in numbers never seen before. The river Thames was alive with traffic, the streets throbbing with processions, followed by feasts and dramatic productions on a religious theme, which the City companies, especially the Skinners, played a leading role in presenting. On the other hand it was a dangerous place. Heavy punishments were inflicted on criminals, executions were commonplace, the jails were full, and even the wealthiest citizen could find himself in the Tower or Newgate.

As Henry VIII and Wolsey established their control, relations between the City and the Court just down the river at Greenwich became fraught, and the most important asset for a young man on his way to a fortune was the ability to survive. Above all, there was the constant fear of sudden epidemics and plagues which struck down large numbers, and led to most of the wealthy having country houses where they could retire when the plague struck. There was a fear of foreigners, generated by worries about jobs, and there was distrust and envy of foreign bankers. On May Day 1517 the apprentices of London rioted against the presence of foreign traders in the City; the Lord Mayor was unable to control the riot, even with the help of the much-loved Sir Thomas More. Finally, arrests were made and the ringleaders executed. Andrew Judde was not involved in this demonstration – he was far too busy.

During these turbulent times Andrew Judde, together with Buknell, his master, must have travelled frequently between London and Calais. Being apprenticed to both the Skinners and the Staplers, he must have learnt both crafts, though it is probable that he was more Stapler than Skinner, at least until he had made his fortune. He is known to have paid customs duty on a cargo in 1517 in his own name, and once he had won his freedom of the Staple he started on his remarkable career, which took him along several paths at the same time.

First, he was a Stapler, with all that meant during this prosperous period for the wool trade. In due course he became Mayor of the Staple. He was Mayor when Philip of Spain spent the night at Calais in 1555 and presented the king with a gift of 1,000 gold marks. He represented the Staplers before the Council in London, protesting about the heavy demands the Council was making on the Staplers, and he was Mayor when Calais fell to the French in 1558. This disaster happened just before his death and may well have precipitated it.

Next, he became a dealer in several other commodities, frequently in partnership with other City magnates like Sir Thomas Gresham. He was very highly regarded as a financier and both arranged loans for Edward VI and lent the young king money himself. Edward VI recorded in his diary that Judde had been swindled out of £1,500 in Antwerp.

Finally, he became a backer of trading voyages, both as a financier and a shipowner. He was a founding member of the Muscovy Company, which sent the first ships to Russia. He also backed voyages to Spain and West Africa, though there is no evidence that he was involved in the slave trade, as several other merchants were.

In spite of his Calais duties he played a full part in London life. He was Master of the Skinners' Company six times, Sheriff of London, an Alderman, and eventually Lord Mayor in 1550–1, after which he was knighted. His year as Lord Mayor coincided with a period of failing crops, rising grain prices and two sudden and vicious devaluations of the currency by the Council. He was summoned to Westminster to be reprimanded for mismanagement, though he could not have been blamed for the failings of others, and he must have been relieved to finish his mayoral year. The Lord Mayor was expected to entertain on a lavish scale; this he did, not in his own house in Bishopsgate, which seems to have been quite a humble dwelling, but in the house of his friend, Sir William Holles. When he was elected Lord Mayor, the Skinners made him a grant of £6 to 'trim his lodgings'.

He married three times and his marriages reflect the closeness of the merchant community. His first wife, Mary Mirfin, was daughter of a former Lord Mayor and Master of the Skinners' Company. By her he had four sons and a daughter. His second wife, Agnes, died childless, while he was Lord Mayor, and Machyn, in his *Diary*, records the pomp of her funeral. His third wife was Mary Langton, the wealthy widow of another Skinner, who had four children by her first marriage and gave Judde another daughter.

He was also treasurer of Bart's Hospital and for a short time Surveyor of all the London hospitals. He was in great demand as a friend and executor of other merchants' wills. Seeing how long it took to travel to Calais and back he must have been an extremely busy man. Like so many men of action, he has not received the same credit as that granted to authors, whose works lived beyond them. Perhaps he foresaw that, and that is why, near the end of his life, he decided to found a school in his native town of Tonbridge.

2

THE FIRST HUNDRED YEARS

The School was built in Mary's day,
A front of stone in a field of hay:
Football then was by law forbid,
And no one cared what the day boys did
Outside the School!

The arms of Sir Andrew Judde.
The boar's head appears in the
arms of Sir Andrew Judde and
the school.

While Andrew Judde was busy making his fortune in London, the town of Tonbridge was decaying. In 1521 the owner of the Castle, Edward Stafford, Duke of Buckingham, was beheaded, as his father Henry, the previous Duke, had been. His crime was being of royal descent, making him a potential threat to Henry VIII. His property, including Tonbridge Castle, was forfeited to the Crown. Viscount Rocheford, father of Anne Boleyn, who lived at Hever, was given the task of repairing the Castle and the bridge and wrote to the Crown surveyor asking for more money to make sure that the masons engaged upon the bridge finished their work. Once it was finished, he wrote, it would be so well done he would not need to trouble the king further in his lifetime. The Castle passed into a succession of hands, until Oliver Cromwell ordered it to be dismantled during the Civil War.

In 1525 Wolsey was looking for funds to endow his new school at Ipswich and his new college at Oxford – Cardinal College – later to be known as Christ Church. A year earlier he had obtained from the Pope a bull enabling him to suppress some of the smaller monasteries and priories; he sent Warham, Archbishop of Canterbury, to Tonbridge to hold a meeting with the local inhabitants to discover whether they would like to have a grammar school for forty boys, with exhibitions to carry them on to Oxford, or would prefer to keep the Priory. The citizens of Tonbridge opted to keep their Priory. Warham reluctantly conveyed this information to an angry Cardinal Wolsey. Tonbridge had thrown away the chance to have a school, and, though Wolsey himself was disgraced and died, the Priory was sold in 1532 and became a ruin.

Whether this fact or his own lack of formal education inspired Andrew

Judde to build a school in Tonbridge will never be known, but his decision to do so reflects the changes taking place in London at that time. On the one hand there was an increased need for schools through the growth of the learned professions, whose language was Latin. On the other, with Luther's ideas gaining ground, the attitude to charity was changing. Even though Henry VIII had written a book condemning Luther in 1521, the move towards removal of all the trappings of catholicism was under way, and this meant the end of rich men leaving their money to monasteries and churches to say masses for their souls.

The Tudor merchants were not short of social conscience, and their wealth, often vast, needed to be spent somewhere. Many of them, including Judde, had profited by the cheap purchase of church lands; their predecessors' desire to leave money for prayers for their own souls was replaced by a feeling that they should help the living. Several, including Judde, established almshouses. Money was given or bequeathed to provide bread and coals for the needy, to help poor maidens marry or to make loans to poor apprentices.

Giving or leaving money to found a school in their home towns was not a new idea. John Sevenoke had founded a free school for poor men's children at Sevenoaks in 1418. Grammar schools were founded in great number during the sixteenth and seventeenth centuries, possibly as many as a thousand, but many of them disappeared within 50 years. Those with the best chance of survival were those with royal charters and the wealthiest founders, and, in particular, those whose founders entrusted their schools to bodies such as City Companies.

Judde must have been thinking about his plan for some time before he set about the lengthy process of obtaining a royal charter. In 1551 he told the Court of the Skinners' Company of his gift of certain lands and houses to establish six almshouses in the ward of St Helen's, Bishopsgate. He said nothing then of his plans for the school, but the Skinners figure significantly in the charter which Edward VI granted the school on 16 May 1553. The charter was in Latin and couched in the long, involved legal language of the time. A copy of it and also an English translation can be found in Rivington. The Latin version covers over five pages and, for all except the dedicated lawyer or historian, is a guaranteed cure for insomnia. It is necessary to reduce it to its main provisions and simplify them:

1. The school shall be called the Free Grammar School of Sir Andrew Judde.

2. The school shall be for the instruction of boys and youth in the said town and the country there adjacent.

3. Sir Andrew Judde during his natural life shall be and be called Governor.

4. After the death of Sir Andrew Judde, the Master, Wardens and Commonalty of the Mistery of the Skinners of London shall be and be called Governors.

No picture or statue of Sir Andrew Judde remains apart from that on his monument. This drawing is an enlargement of his figure in that monument.

The Foundation Stone over the Headmaster's front door. The Foundation Stone was moved to its present position in 1864. The words on it read: THIS : SHOLE : MADE : BI : SIR : ANDRO : IWDE : KNIGHT : AND : GEVIN : TO : THE : COMPANE : OF : SKINERS : ANO : 1553.

5. Sir Andrew Judde, and after his death the Governors, shall have the power of appointing the Master and Under Master.

6. They shall have power to make fit and wholesome statutes for the direction of the Master and Under Master and Scholars.

7. They shall seek the advice of the Warden and Fellows of the College of All Souls in the University of Oxford concerning the statutes.

8. They shall have the power to buy and sell property to the yearly value of forty pounds.

Having obtained the charter, Judde set about building the school, appointing the first Headmaster and writing the statutes, though in which order is not known. His eldest brother, Thomas, had died, leaving his Tonbridge property to Andrew's nephew, Henry, who was very close to his uncle. Among Henry's property was the estate known as Houselands, and it is probable that the site on which Judde built the school was part of it. The Judde lands in Tonbridge were later sold, apart from the three acres on which the school was built to the west of the High Street, just north of the town fosse.

Whether the building was completed before the school opened, or whether the school was started elsewhere and moved in when the building was ready, is unknown, but the building seems to have been planned and executed with some speed, and a very attractive building it was. Built of Kentish sandstone, it stood just back from the main road (*see* page 22). It was 160 feet long and 25 feet wide, with a bell turret in the middle. The Headmaster's house was at the south end and the Usher's much smaller house at the north end. In between were the schoolroom, about 40 feet long, the dining-room and the kitchen. The dormitories were on the upper floor.

The first Headmaster was the Revd. John Proctor, a fellow of All Souls College. He was an ardent catholic, or at least an ardent supporter of Queen Mary, and it must have been difficult for Judde to decide whether to appoint a catholic or a protestant. We do not know Judde's religious beliefs – like most of his friends, he was a survivor and trimmed his views to suit the volatile mood of the day. He had been close to finding himself in disgrace in 1553, when, as an adviser of Edward VI and the Protector, Northumberland, he had been a signatory of Edward's will, by which Northumberland had persuaded the dying king to bequeath the crown to his young cousin, Lady Jane Grey. When Mary successfully claimed the crown, Northumberland and Lady Jane were executed, but somehow Judde and his friends exculpated themselves and pledged their allegiance to Mary.

The school probably opened in the latter part of 1553, and soon after both Judde and the new Headmaster were involved in the next major event of Queen Mary's reign. There was widespread feeling in the country, particularly in Kent, against Mary, for planning to marry a Spaniard. At the end of 1553 the terms of her marriage to Philip of Spain were

8

proclaimed, and a large group of Kentish gentlemen, under the leadership of Sir Thomas Wyat, planned a rebellion. The rebels met in groups in Tonbridge and other towns, before moving off to join up for the march on London. John Proctor, rushed out of his study into the High Street, grabbed one of the rebels' bridles and tried to stop them. The rebels ignored him and marched off.

The army sent by the queen to resist the rebels deserted to Wyat's cause, but Wyat's army had only one way into London from Southwark, and that was over London Bridge. There on the bridge stood the Lord Admiral, the Lord Mayor, Sir Thomas White, and his great friend and supporter, Sir Andrew Judde. Having withdrawn behind the drawbridge, these gentlemen ordered it to be raised, and Wyat's route into London was blocked. The rebels marched away to Kingston to cross the river and approach London along the north bank, but they were defeated and the leaders executed. However, that is not the end of the story from the Tonbridge point of view. Proctor returned to his study and wrote a book on the uprising, *A Historie of Wyates Rebellion*, which became a kind of official history and earned Proctor an entry in the *Dictionary of National Biography*, in which Andrew Judde, for all his achievements, never attained a place. Proctor, not surprisingly, dedicated his book to Queen Mary: there is a copy of it in the school library.

From 1553 until his death in 1558 Judde was the sole Governor of the school, and, at some time, he framed the statutes which were to govern it for the next 270 years.

The statutes of most of the schools founded at this time are remarkably similar. Founders and Governors borrowed freely from each other and no doubt there were lawyers doing a booming business in statute framing. Tonbridge's statutes are said to be based on Dean Colet's statutes for St Paul's, whereas Oundle paid 12 pence for the loan of Tonbridge's statutes.

The statutes are lengthy and mostly obvious, and copies of them in Latin and English are in Rivington. To reduce them to palatable form, they decreed:

The Master should be paid £20 per annum and the Usher £8.

Both should have free lodgings.

Both should be medically and morally fit for the job.

They should not be gamblers or haunters of taverns.

The Masters should be allowed to take twelve boarders and the Usher eight.

The townspeople should benefit financially by being able to take boarders.

No boy should be allowed to enter the school who could not write competently and read perfectly in Latin and English.

Each boy entering the school should pay sixpence into the Common Box.

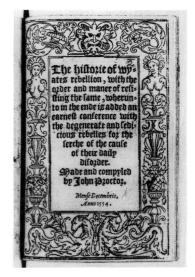

John Proctor, the first Headmaster, achieved brief fame as a historian with his Historie of Wyates rebellion *written in 1554, one year after the school opened. The school's copy of the original was stolen at an exhibition and this photo of the title page is from the replica in the school Library.*

The Common Box. *All pupils entering the school had to pay sixpence for books. Fines were also payable for absence. The Governors suspected Tommy Roots of dishonesty and provided a box with a key which they kept. The OT Masonic Lodge has one of the old boxes; the other, shown here, is in the school Library and is presumably the one which locked.*

Each boy being absent without good excuse should pay one penny for each day's absence into the Common Box.

Work on weekdays should begin and end with prayers.

Hours should be from 7 a.m. until 11 a.m. then from 1 p.m. until 5 p.m. in winter and 6 p.m. in summer.

Extra holidays should not be granted more than four times a year.

The boys and at least one master should attend the parish church on Sundays and Holy Days.

Detailed instructions were also given about how the Visitation by the Governors should be conducted. Surprisingly, nowhere does it say that the Governors should attend, but it is decreed that on Visitation Day there should be disputations, lasting from one o'clock till evensong. The vicar should judge the disputations and award the three prize pens to the best three disputers. Disputations were much in vogue at the time and were an idea copied from St Paul's School. The subjects to be disputed were chosen by the Headmaster and some of them must have been very tedious. When these were over, the school should process to the church, with the three prize-winners with garlands on their heads at the back, just in front of the Master and the Usher. The church service should begin with prayers for the monarch and end with prayers for the founder.

One point in the statutes needs considering. First, they make it very clear that Tonbridge, unlike most of the other free schools, was to be a boarding school, and that the townspeople should benefit financially from taking boarders. It was not intended to be just a school where all the townspeople's sons could receive free education. In any case Tonbridge town was simply not big enough to provide boys to fill a school clearly designed to take 60 boys. From the outset it was probably meant to take up to 50 boarders and about 10 day boys.

Boys were to be taught Latin, English, a little Greek and possibly Hebrew. Most of this teaching would have been of little use to the local tradesmen's sons, and the argument about what Judde meant by 'free' education has continued ever since. The bulk of opinion has concluded that 'free' was merely a word commonly put in front of grammar school, and that it meant free from outside jurisdiction and not free of cost.

At the beginning of September 1558 Andrew Judde was taken ill, possibly with one of the plagues then so prevalent. On 2 September he signed his will and died a day or two later. On 14 September he was buried with great pomp in St Helen's, Bishopsgate. His funeral is described in detail in Machyn's *Diary*.

At some later date before 1600 his memorial tablet was set into the wall of St Helen's Church. The epitaph is of poor literary quality and gives details of his life which simply could not have been true. It does not do justice to a man of such remarkable energy and versatility, but it is the only epitaph we have. Surprisingly, the epitaph does not mention the school.

Sir Andrew Judde's monument in St Helen's Church, Bishopsgate, 1558. It is thought that the monument was erected up to 50 years after his death. His epitaph below contains some facts which are known to be inaccurate. Historians regard the quality of the English as unworthy of him:
TO RVSSIA AND MVSCOVA TO SPAYNE GVNNY WITHOVTE FABLE TRAVELD HE BY LAND AND SEA BOTHE MAYRE OF LONDON AND STAPLE THE COMMONWELTHE HE NORISHED SO WORTHELIE IN ALL HIS DAIES THAT ECH STATE FVLLWELL HIM LOVED TO HIS PERPETVALL PRAYES THREE WYVES HE HAD ONE WAS MARY FOWER SYNES ONE MAYDE HAD HE BY HER ANNYS HAD NONE BY HIM TRVLY BY DAME MARY HAD ONE DOWGHTER THVS IN THE MONTH OF SEPTEMBER A THOWSANDE FYVE HVNDRED FYFTEY AND EYGHT DIED THIS WORTHIE STAPLAR WORSHIPYNGE HIS POSTERYTE.

'The Grammar School, Tunbridge, Kent', by T. M. Baynes, 1826. This is one of the best-known pictures of the school. It shows the school just after the Lower School was built in 1826 but before Cawthorn's Library was enlarged to match the new wing.

When he purchased the land and houses to endow the school, he bought them jointly in the name of himself and his friend and servant, Henry Fisher, with the intention that they should transfer them to the Skinners' Company before his death, but they failed to do so. Henry Fisher was no ordinary servant, but a fellow Skinner and Stapler, and servant was a word used then for apprentice or junior partner. Unfortunately, Judde's will was finished in a hurry, and in it he left to the Skinners the same property which he then owned in partnership with Fisher, forgetting that it was no longer his sole property to bequeath. He also bequeathed extra property not mentioned in his earlier plans.

Fisher carried out his part of the bargain and transferred the joint property to the Skinners and made extra bequests of his own to the school, but the complexities of these arrangements led to several legal cases, most of them in the next 70 years, but some of them as late as 1820. Fisher's son, Andrew, claimed that some of the property belonged to him, and it needed two Acts of Parliament in 1572 and 1589 to confirm the school in its possessions. It is said that the Skinners spent £4,000 of their own money in defending the school during these years, far more than the income of the estates Judde had transferred. Many schools foundered because of such legal problems. The Skinners' Company could not have done more to fulfil Judde's confidence in them – so much so that when Sir Wolstan Dixie, seven times Master of the Skinners' Company, died in 1593 and left £700 to the Company in trust for founding a grammar school at Market Bosworth, the Skinners refused the bequest!

One outcome of the battle between Andrew Fisher and the Skinners was that the statutes were submitted to Parker, Archbishop of Canterbury, and Nowell, Dean of St Paul's, for approval. Judde had decreed that boys should only be allowed four extra holidays a year. The Dean changed this to once a week and wrote at the bottom 'I have perused these statutes and like them well'. The Archbishop altered his amendment and said holidays (remedies) should only be given once a fortnight. Otherwise the statutes were approved.

For the next 100 years few details of the school survive apart from rare entries in the Skinners' records, mainly those concerning the appointment of a new Master, the Visitation and the cost of repairs. Money spent on repairs was surprisingly little and mainly concerns small items such as providing a table for the schoolroom, building a brew-house with oven for the Usher, paying for the foundation stone to be made and set into the wall of the Master's house and supplying a new bell.

A list of Headmasters for these years can be found in Rivington. Proctor died in 1558, the same year as Judde and Queen Mary, and was buried in the parish church. His successors were usually clergymen; all were classical scholars and they nearly all wrote books, sometimes for the use of their pupils. What we know about them is very limited, and it is only worth mentioning a few of the facts we do have.

The Revd. John Stockwood (1547–87) wrote a grammar book for school

Opposite top. 'The 1832 Election', by C. T. Dodd sen. Dodd painted this picture when he was only 17, two years before he became Drawing Master. His early style seems surprisingly modern. Elections in those days always led to lively scenes in the High Street around the old Town Hall, seen from the north side, and now pulled down. Polling was held in the open and lasted three days. Vicesimus Knox II and Thomas Knox were both keen on politics and their radical views did little to increase numbers at the school. Homersham Cox, founder of a dynasty still represented at the school, and an eminent barrister, wrote a book titled Antient Elections *based on his memories of these elections while he was a boy at the school.*

Opposite bottom. 'A View of the Grammar School at Tonbridge in Kent', by Jonah Smith Wells, 1831. Jonah Smith Wells was Master of the Skinners' Company, and presented this picture to Skinners' Hall, where it still hangs. The carriage in the picture is probably that of the Governors arriving for Skinners' Day.

This silver flagon was one of many presents taken to the Tsar Boris Godunov by Sir Thomas Smythe in 1604.

use which was still being used in schools in the eighteenth century: when he became vicar of Tonbridge, he was asked to resign by the Governors, who said that he could not do both jobs at once. When he left, there was competition for the post and the Governors appointed a committee of six to choose his successor, the Revd. William Hatch (1587–1615), the first OT Headmaster. By then the school's reputation seems to have been well established, as Holinshed's *Chronicle*, published in 1577, after talking of Judde's foundation of the school, says that therein he 'brought up and nourished in lerning grete store of youth as well bred in Kent as brought up in other counties adjoining'.

One of Holinshed's assistants was Francis Thynne, a famous antiquary, who must have been in the school when it opened or soon after. As he was the son of the Master of Henry VIII's·household, Judde's desire to attract the sons of gentry seems to have met with instant success.

According to the Skinners' records, the Revd. Michael Jenkins (1615–24) was appointed because 'he was the only one who turned up'. During his reign the school benefited greatly from further generous endowments from Sir Thomas Smythe, son of Andrew Judde's daughter Alice. Alice had married Thomas Smythe, Customer of London, a wealthy haberdasher who was also a Merchant of Muscovy and collector of the Queen's Customs for the Port of London. The second of her 13 children, Thomas, also a customs collector and an extremely wealthy man, made his home at Southborough and left several benefactions to the poor of Bidborough and Tonbridge. Life was still not easy for the top men in London; Smythe was accused of treason and imprisoned briefly in the Tower, but he survived and became Founder of the Virginia Company and Governor of both the East India and Muscovy Companies as well as special Ambassador to Russia.

Smythe raised the Master's and the Usher's salaries by 50 per cent – a very necessary step in days when inflation was beginning to hurt. He founded six Smythe exhibitions of ten pounds in value and seven years in duration to enable Tonbridge boys to go to university with a view to taking orders. We still have a record of the candidates for these exhibitions in 1621. They included:

> Thomas Smith – a boy whose parents were 'of small abilitie' (wealth);
> John Dixon – a boy whose friends were 'of great abilitie' – they held Hilden Manor;
> John Large – a minister's son;
> Geo. Children – a very poor woman's son.

Names from the Large and Children families appeared in the school lists right up to recent generations.

Thomas Horne (1640–9) was a staunch Parliamentarian and in 1649 was rewarded by being promoted to the Headmastership of Eton, to replace Dr Grey, who had just been sacked for his royalist views. Grey was out of work, and the Governors promptly appointed him to Tonbridge, where he stayed until he returned to Eton at the Restoration. During Horne's time at the school in 1643, the town saw a small battle, resulting in the death of a soldier outside Ferox Hall, then a private house. The boys missed the excitement as they were on holiday, but for 250 years the story of the Ferox Hall ghost persisted, ostensibly that of a soldier fleeing from his pursuers, knocking on the old front door of Ferox. There is some argument as to whether the ghost is a Cavalier or a Roundhead.

Grey's successor, the Revd. John Goad (1660–2) only stayed two years before moving on to Merchant Taylors'. He was James II's adviser on the weather, though in those days that meant presenting a monthly report of what the weather had been rather than forecasting it. During his time at Tonbridge he was secretly converted to catholicism, a sin which was to earn him the sack from Merchant Taylors' many years later.

Finally in this period, we come to the Revd. Christopher Wase (1662–8). He went to Eton and King's College, Cambridge, where he was deprived of his fellowship for royalist sympathies and forced to flee to the Continent. He served with the Spanish army against the French in Flanders, and was captured. On his release, he made his way to Paris, where the famous diarist, Evelyn, found him in dire straits. Evelyn brought him back to England and became his patron. It may have been Evelyn who obtained for him the Headmastership of Tonbridge. Wase was a very able man and left Tonbridge to enter government service, again with Evelyn's help.

Although Judde had decreed in the statutes that Headmasters should keep and submit annually a list of those at the school, these records are missing, and the first list we have is for 1654. The list for 1665 shows that there were 53 boys in the school, several of them from good Kentish families.

During Wase's headmastership, on Skinners' Day 1665, Evelyn visited the school and recorded the fact in his diary. 'I went to Tunbridge to see a solemn exercise at the Free Schoole there.' By solemn exercise he meant the Skinners' Day disputations which were still held as instructed by the founder. The Governors had not missed a Visitation since 1559. It must have been a terrible burden for some of the older and fatter Governors – a 40-mile journey each way on horseback. The old records list every penny spent on the visit – most of it on drink; apparently they used to camp for the night on Sevenoaks Common. Now they reside in great luxury at the Rose and Crown Hotel and bring their own drink with them. However, one should not begrudge the Governors what little luxury they allow themselves. In the Great Fire of London in 1666 the school houses in Gracechurch Street were all burnt to the ground. The Governors, to make up for the loss of rents on which the school was so dependent, decreed that they should 'for the present hold no feasts or entertainments, and devote the sum thereby saved to the support of the School'.

So the school completed its first 100 years with roughly the same number of boys with which it started. Sir Andrew Judde's faith in his beloved Skinners' Company had been more than justified.

13

3

THE SECOND HUNDRED YEARS

Now good King Charles·he loved good cheer,
He came to Tonbridge every year:
He drank the waters to mend his health,
He watched the cricket to please himself –
He knew the School!

Even though we know that Evelyn visited the school, there is no evidence that Charles II did, as Clemence Dane implies in verse three of her song above, though he probably visited Summer Hill, just outside Tonbridge, where his sister often stayed.

Nor is there any record of cricket at Tonbridge in this century. Clemence Dane may have been fantasizing, but many of her lines contain a germ of truth, and it is infuriating that her verse can be neither proved nor disproved.

On Wase's departure, the loss of two headmasters in such a short time may have made the Governors decide to opt for someone less ambitious. In any case, Wase, recommended his Usher, Thomas Roots, who, having been born in Tonbridge and educated at the school, might be less inclined to move on. He became Headmaster in 1668 and remained for 46 years. The Governors' wish for a long headmastership was granted with a vengeance. They spent the last 30 years trying to get rid of him.

Somervell is rather unkind about Roots and his long headmastership, but Thomas Knox, a later Headmaster, in his own short history of the school, says that Roots was no scholar but had very acceptable attainments, though Thomas Knox may have been biased because he was a direct descendant of Roots through his mother. Christopher Wase thought highly enough of Roots, not only to recommend him for the headmastership, but later, when he was working for the government in London, to send his own son to Tonbridge, rather than to one of the four famous London schools.

There is very little written material about the school over the next 100 years, and the best that can be said is that it survived, while dozens, if not hundreds, of similar schools failed. Many of them were restrained by their

TO GOD ONLY BEE ALL GLORY

THIS GALLERY WAS ERECTED BY THE
WORSHIPFVLL COMPANYE OF SKYNNERS WITH
THE FREE CONSENT OF THIS PARISH FOR THE
VSE OF THEIR SCHOLL FOR EVER ANNO 1663

This coat of arms originally hung on the gallery used by the boys in the parish church. When the gallery was pulled down in 1879, it was presented to the school and now hangs above the entrance to the Skinners' Library.

statutes from raising the salaries of the Headmasters and Ushers, and no one could be found to teach on the miserable salaries fixed a hundred years earlier. Sir Thomas Smythe had raised the Tonbridge salaries by 50 per cent, and in addition the Governors traditionally paid the Headmaster and Usher a gratuity.

Numbers fluctuated between 40 and 90, and, within the next 100 years, the school obtained a new refectory and a new library, both of which implied confidence in the future. The school during most of this time was well thought of by the local clergy and gentry and was able to boast a few Old Boys who were to become eminent, particularly Thomas Herbert, later Earl of Pembroke, master and embellisher of Wilton House and holder of many of the highest offices of state, and Charles Mordaunt, later Earl of Peterborough, the general who captured Barcelona in the War of the Spanish Succession. Both Herbert and Mordaunt came to the school because of Wase or possibly Evelyn, for Wase had been tutor to Herbert's eldest brother, while Evelyn was an adviser to the Mordaunt family. The Earl of Pembroke always remained loyal to Tonbridge and Thomas Roots in particular. It is not certain that Mordaunt came to Tonbridge, though he later became Master of the Skinners, and it is not possible to check from his diary because his widow burnt it as being too scandalous for preservation.

Roots certainly took over at a difficult time, not so much for the school as for the Governors. The Great Fire of London had not only destroyed Skinners' Hall, and with it some of the documents which might have made the writing of this book easier, but also the houses in the City from which the school drew its rents. The Governors found it impossible to fulfil the various clauses of the Judde and Smythe bequests. The funds for bread money for the poor and for Smythe exhibitions was severely curtailed, and even they had to be subsidized from the Skinners' own funds.

In his early years, Roots seems to have been quite successful and, up until 1681, there were favourable reports on the school either from the examiner or the Master of the Skinners.

In 1672 the Court minutes record: 'Scholars increased in numbers. Clergymen and Gentlemen of the County much commended the Schoolmaster and Scholars.'

However, throughout his time Roots was at loggerheads with the local residents, with whom he may have. been unpopular because he was regarded as a jumped-up local lad. In 1671 he became involved in the most extraordinary squabble with a local magistrate, Thomas Lambarde of Sevenoaks. This episode is worth mentioning, not only for its insight into Roots's character, but also for the quaint language of the time. Mr Lambarde wrote to the Governors complaining of Roots on several grounds: (1) He had accused the Governors of cheating the school and the town over Sir Thomas Smythe's charity. (2) He had organized the elopement of his own sister with Lambarde's son. (3) He had for several days been at Sevenoaks, away from his duties at Tonbridge. (4) He was a haunter of taverns and on one occasion had got beastly drunk. (5) He had invited Lambarde's sons to drinking sessions and coursing matches and to steal venison.

The Governors asked Roots for an explanation and his long letter of self-justification can be seen at Skinners' Hall. He swore that he had never said anything disrespectful about the Governors; that Lambarde's son had been the prime instigator in his elopement with Roots's sister; that he had not been in Sevenoaks more than three days in his life, and that he never left the school without appointing a deputy; that he had been to a tavern, but only with a prospective parent. Here is one paragraph from the letter:

> I had (I confess) bin at the Tavern and drank freely (but not to debauch) with Mr Worge a Gentleman of Bourne in Sussex and his wife and son-in-law, who then brought a son to schoole. Nor have I had the advantage of disburdening a charg'd stomach that way, for five years.

Finally he half admitted the poaching charge:

> However, since my dogs gave occasion of scandall, I have given them away with an inviolate resolution never to keep more.

The Governors accepted Roots's explanation and wrote to Lambarde that they were 'fully satisfied of the Abilities of the said Mr Rootes'.

One cannot help smiling at the thought of some of our recent Headmasters being accused of these crimes or lurking round Hayesden trying to poach a deer.

For some years the Governors continued to be happy with Roots's performance. A refectory was added behind the school building in 1676, and in 1679 the school was provided with a new front fence, the bakery was retiled, the pump repaired and 'some dark chambers enlightened'. The visiting Governors continued to express their satisfaction at the state of the school and recommend payment of the traditional annual gratuity to the Headmaster.

However, from 1680 the numbers started to decline, and for several years the examiners reported that there were no candidates fit for university. Roots even wrote to the Governors asking them to dispense with the Visitation, as there were no boys fit to be examined in public. The Governors declined his request. If boarding numbers dropped, it became more important to woo the day-boy population, and the Governors came to Tonbridge to dine with the local inhabitants and find out why the school was so unpopular. It appeared that the unpopularity of the school rested with the Headmaster, who had raised the entrance fees illegally. The town had even imposed rates on the school for the first time and Roots had had his goods distrained when he refused to pay the rate.

The townspeople claimed that the Headmaster kept them in the dark about their rights to free education under the Founder's will, and they were assured that a copy of the statutes would be kept available for public inspection in the school library. The Governors had to send to Roots for a copy of the statutes, and it can only be assumed that their own copy was lost in the Fire of London. As the Governors themselves had to keep consulting counsel about the meaning of the statutes, it is not surprising the townspeople were confused.

For the last 30 years of his headmastership, the Governors made half-hearted attempts to remove Roots from his post. They withheld his gratuity; they refused to pay his repair bills; they offered him an increased gratuity if he would retire. On one occasion he appealed for help to his old pupil the Earl of Pembroke, then Lord Privy Seal, who summoned the Governors to Westminster to state their case.

In 1705 the Governors refused to grant Roots's son a Smythe exhibition unless Roots promised to resign. In 1710 they replaced the old Common Box with an iron box with a key which they kept and emptied once a year. Nevertheless Roots survived their combination of rebukes, bribes and threats. Numbers declined badly in his later years, and though the school list for 1714 contained 32 names, only 14 answered their names at the Visitation, the rest having left during the year. When Roots died in 1714, there must have been intense relief all round. The Governors needed to find the right man to restore the school's fortunes.

The man they chose, the Revd. Richard Spencer, was an MA of King's College, Cambridge, who was vicar of Cobham in East Kent. He was known to the Governors, as he had been the All Souls examiner and preacher at a recent Visitation.

Spencer was an immediate success and raised the numbers of the school rapidly. He was clearly popular with the local gentry, and boys came flooding in. By 1721 numbers had risen to over 70, and the school list for that year contains boys from several well-known Kent families. The Governors expressed their satisfaction with Spencer by raising his annual gratuity to 30 guineas. Several of his pupils went on to successful careers and included a future Lord Mayor of London and a vice-chancellor of Cambridge University, as well as George Austen, the father of Jane Austen.

From now on we have most of the school lists, from which we can see that for seven years out of 11, between 1727 and 1737, one of Spencer's sons was Head Boy, a position held by the cleverest boy. His family, however, brought him a great deal of grief. He lost his wife quite early, then his elder son, then his daughter. Perhaps he lost heart, for numbers declined at the end of his reign. Hart regards him as one of the most successful of our Headmasters, and it is a great pity that we do not have more written evidence to justify this claim. Perhaps the following paragraph is indicative of growing affection for the school or for Spencer.

On 8 June 1744, the following advert appeared in the *Daily Advertiser*: 'The Gentlemen educated at Tonbridge School are desired to dine at the Fountain Tavern in Bartholomew's Lane, on Monday next, 11th instant. Note. Dinner to be on the table at two o'clock.'

This is possibly the first written record of an Old Boys' dinner in London of any school, but surprisingly neither Rivington nor Somervell mentions it.

On Spencer's resignation in 1743, half the 52 boys in the school also left. This may have been coincidence, or it may have been that the local gentry were apprehensive about the Governors' next appointment, for surprisingly the man they chose was only 23 years old. The Revd. James Cawthorn was not only very young, he was a blunt Yorkshireman as well. For many years after his death he was the best-known Tonbridge Headmaster, not because of his ability, which was probably considerable, but because of his ghost, whose legend survived for a long time.

Why the Governors found him worthy of being appointed Headmaster of Tonbridge at such a young age is not clear. He had little experience of teaching, but had acquired some fame as a poet. He lost his children in infancy and his young wife soon after, and his most memorable poem is one entitled 'A Father's Extempore Consolation' about the loss of a child. Perhaps his bereavements caused him to be severe, for he had a formidable reputation for severity, in the mould of Keate of Eton and Busby of Westminster, whereas nearly all the other Headmasters mentioned in this book were mild men. His reputation for severity does not seem to fit with his passion for music and poetry. He was reputed to have been a great lover of music and was also fond of riding, though a poor horseman. He was in the habit of riding to London for a concert in the evening and returning in time for morning school.

It is hard to think of such a man as being as bad as other histories have painted him. He was described as 'being hard in School matters and pleasant in Society' – not a bad reputation for a Headmaster in those days.

Anyway, school numbers started to rise soon after his arrival, and many of his pupils went on to achieve fame. One of them, Sampson Gideon, was made a baronet while still a boy at school. His father was a Jewish financier, whose advice had been particularly useful to George II. As Jews could not then receive titles, the king bestowed the title on young Sampson who was a Christian.

Also at school under Cawthorn were George Austen, father of Jane Austen, and William Woodfall. George Austen returned to the school as Usher, before he moved to his living in Hampshire, where Jane was born. William Woodfall, known as 'Memory' Woodfall and regarded as the father of parliamentary reporting, was known for his memory even at school. Cawthorn once set him a book of Homer to learn, and he recited it perfectly the next morning, causing Cawthorn to burst into tears. Woodfall went on to report the debates in the House of Commons, where journalists were not allowed to take notes, and produced word-perfect reports in his paper the next day.

Cawthorn persuaded the Governors to build a library next to the south end of the school in 1760. It was a building of classical design, later incorporated into the nineteenth-century developments and used as a combined library and dining-room for the Headmaster. It was known for some time as Cawthorn's Library and later as the Skinners' Library.

In 1761 Cawthorn died from a riding accident, aged 41. He stopped on Quarry Hill to let his horse drink from a trough, fell off and broke his leg. He died a few days later. The story is that the accident happened as he was hurrying back to school to release a boy whom he had locked in a cupboard and forgotten. The boy was found dead, and, if he himself had not died, Cawthorn must have been charged with manslaughter. This, however, hardly damaged his reputation, as is shown by the large number of local subscribers to his published poems. This tragedy gave birth to the school's favourite ghost story. The legend of Cawthorn's ghost haunting the School House dormitories ensured that he was remembered for over a hundred years. The legend was so strong that a maid had to sit up in the dormitory that night every year.

There were 67 boys in the school when the Governors appointed another North countryman, the Revd. Johnson Towers, aged 37. As he had lived in Kent for several years and been Usher at the school (1747–58) numbers did not drop, and during his years as Headmaster the school experienced a period of steady, if uneventful, prosperity, with numbers remaining at around 65. Towers seems to have been an equable man, for when his house in Westmorland was occupied by rebel soldiers during the 1745 rebellion, he remarked that it would save him the cost of looking after it during the winter. His son, also called Johnson, was at the school.

In 1765 the town again raised the question of 'free education', and the Governors asked a panel of eminent lawyers, including Blackstone, to decide who was entitled to benefit from the free education the school was meant to offer. The lawyers decided that the inhabitants of the parish of

Sampson Gideon, Bt., artist and date unknown. Sir Sampson Gideon, later Lord Eardley of Spalding (1744–1824) was created a baronet by George II while still a boy at the school, because his father, also called Sampson, had given successful financial advice to the Duke of Newcastle, Pitt's business manager. Father Sampson was a Jew and could not be honoured, but his son was a Christian and could. By coincidence, the Duke of Newcastle and his brother, Henry Pelham, both Prime Ministers under George II, were sons of an Old Tonbridgian.

Tonbridge had the right to have their children, who could write competently and read Latin and English perfectly, instructed in grammar learning at the school without paying any fee except the sixpence entrance fee.

The Governors passed a resolution and sent a copy to the Headmaster and to the Vestry Clerk, Thomas Scoones (OT) who had the resolution inscribed on a board and posted in the porch of the parish church where it hangs still.

Unfortunately this period of the school's history is woefully short of written material, but there do survive letters between Towers and the Bishop of Rochester which at least give us some idea of the real cost of a boarder's education at that time. The Bishop of Rochester had enquired about sending his great-nephew to the school and asked about fees etc.

Towers replied with a flowery, rather sycophantic letter saying that the fees were as follows:

Board & Classical Learning	£20. 0. 0 pr anm
French if learnt	£2. 2. 0 Do
Writing & accts.	£1. 4. 9 Do
Dancing if learnt	£2. 15. 0 Do
Latn. usher at Xtmass	10. 6
Servts. do	10. 6

Towers explains that 'I find it necessary to have a French master in the house, and a dancing-master attends the school from London once a week. . . . There is a very good writing-master in the town greatly under my own direction.'

Obviously satisfied, the Bishop accepted the offer on behalf of his relative, which was a great compliment to the school because, ten years earlier, while he was Dean of Westminster, the Bishop had, in a sermon, lavished praise on Westminster School. That he could now recommend Tonbridge for his great-nephew suggests a high reputation for Tonbridge under Towers. Accepting the offer, the Bishop wrote that the boy's father would pay £25 per annum instead of £20, to which Towers replied that in that case more than ordinary care should be taken of the boy, who should be treated as his own son.

Unfortunately Towers died at the age of 48, during the Christmas holidays 1771. The mid-sevententh century had seen the fortunes of the school restored by three able Headmasters, but the last two died before their full potential could be fulfilled, and the stormy days of the French Revolution lay ahead.

4

THE THREE KNOXES

Mr Knox of Tunbridge has a new coach just come out spick and span with a pair of long tail grays. Is this not quite the thing? My aunt says, 'Lor' Sir, a schoolmaster's is a vast fine trade.'

Boy's letter home, 1781

In 1772, when the Revd. Vicesimus Knox, the Second Master of Merchant Taylors' School was appointed Headmaster, the school had made a steady recovery from the disastrous reign of Tommy Roots, but it was not yet set for the major leap forward which some other schools were already making. The fates, however, were preparing the ground.

The town of Tonbridge, which for 200 years had been as sleepy as the school, had already started to stir. A bill was passed in 1739 to make the Medway navigable from Tonbridge down to the sea, and the Medway Company formed. Work started immediately, and the river was open for traffic by 1741.

Tonbridge wharf was to become an important loading-point for the timbers needed for the Navy, and for produce for the London market. At the same time, Tonbridge became an important unloading-point for previously unobtainable materials, and the new availability of chalk and lime enabled the old-style houses in the area to be replaced by brick ones.

Tonbridge was also on the main road from London to Rye, still the favourite port for Continental travel, and traffic was quite heavy. The turnpike system, which became general in the seventeenth century, brought about a great improvement in the state of the roads, and when stage-coaches became common in the 1790s, Tonbridge became a hub in the stage-coach network, and up to 30 stage-coaches a day rattled through the town. This stage-coach system lasted only 70 years, but it was to be replaced, in the 1840s, by a new system of transport – the railways – which was to help both the town and school to a remarkable extent. Somervell claims, 'No school in England was so affected by the building of the railway.'

When Vicesimus Knox, a distinguished classical scholar, arrived in 1772, it is doubtful if he gave much thought to the question of transport or

A small watercolour of Vicesimus Knox II, copied anonymously from a portrait in oils by Archer James Oliver and exhibited at the Royal Academy in 1809.

21

'Grammar School at Tunbridge, Kent.' One of two pictures showing the original school building, already 200 years old, though the artist and date are unknown. The building on the left has too high a roof to be Cawthorn's Library which had an almost flat roof, and perhaps pre-dates that building.

realized the importance it was to play in the future of the school. Nor could he have foreseen that he was about to create a dynasty of Headmasters almost unique in public school history. His son and his grandson were to follow him as Headmaster. By the time his grandson, Thomas Knox, died in 1843, many of the changes mentioned above were in full swing, and the school was well placed to prosper.

Vicesimus Knox was Headmaster for only six years. During his short reign numbers dropped to 17, of whom only eight were boarders; the boys ranged in age from eight to 19, all taught in the same room at the same time. Knox retired at the age of 49 because of ill-health and died almost immediately. He was the third successive headmaster to die while still in his forties, and this was a blow which most schools would find hard to take. The Governors, however, did not have to look far for his replacement.

In 1779, they appointed his elder son, confusingly also called Vicesimus. He went to Merchant Taylors' and then to St John's College, Oxford, where he studied classics and won fame as a composer of Latin verses. He spent four more years studying English Literature and became a friend of Oliver Goldsmith. He wrote a book of essays which was sent to Dr Johnson for his comments. Dr Johnson praised it highly and forecast a bright future for its author. It was published under the title *Essays, Moral and Literary*, ran to several editions, was translated into most European languages and became very popular in American universities. It was said to have had a wider readership than any publication apart from *The Spectator*. Such was his reputation at Oxford, that several of the top figures at Oxford made strenuous efforts to dissuade him from coming to Tonbridge.

School numbers under the young Vicesimus rose to 85, and pupils started to arrive from all over England and also from the West Indies, simply on the strength of his reputation. Disraeli's father applied to come to Tonbridge at the late age of 19 and live with Knox, but the plan was not fulfilled.

Knox had his human side. Worried by ill-health, he drank the waters from the Tonbridge spring on Quarry Hill, rendered palatable by blending them with port wine. He was also able to enjoy a satisfactory life-style, as the letter quoted above from a boy to his father shows.

Alas, from the school's point of view, there is often a price to pay if its Headmaster becomes a national figure. Knox was a famous preacher, a man of strong opinions and an ardent believer in civil liberties. Initially a fervent supporter of the French Revolution, he sided with Fox in his opposition to the allied attack on France. In 1793 he preached a sermon at St Nicholas Church in Brighton on the evils of war. Brighton contained a large Army garrison and many of the officers and their ladies attended that church. Fans fluttered and boots scraped as the Headmaster of Tonbridge took as his text 'Peace on earth, goodwill towards men'. A few days later, when attending a play at the Brighton theatre, he was spotted in one of the boxes with his family; the officers stood up and caused such a riot that they forced him to leave the theatre. *The Times* reported the incident and school numbers dropped.

However, it is not without irony that several Old Tonbridgians were to make their names in the Napoleonic Wars that followed.

Sir Sidney Smith was Commodore in command of the British forces at Acre in 1799 when they defeated Napoleon. Sidney Smith had an extraordinary career in America, Sweden, the Near East and Italy, and Napoleon regarded him as one of the chief causes of his failure.

It was an OT, Lord Whitworth, who was British Ambassador in Paris during the Peace of Amiens. When Napoleon wished to restart hostilities, he twice insulted Lord Whitworth. Lord Whitworth later returned to Knole, and raised his own battalion of 600 infantry, known as the Holmesdale battalion. In 1813 he became Viceroy of Ireland.

During the Peace of Amiens another OT came to see how the school and Vicesimus Knox were surviving the War. Hardly surprising, except that the OT in question was one of Napoleon's generals, Pierre Dumoustier. He had played a key role in Napoleon's victory at the battle of Marengo and was later to have a long, distinguished military career. As the battles of Acre and Marengo happened in the same year – 1799 – this means that within months of S. Smith (OT) successfully defending Acre against Napoleon, P. Dumoustier (OT) was helping Napoleon win Marengo.

Knox retired in 1812, moved to London and died in 1821. A very large crowd attended his funeral, and there is a monument to him in the parish church. Numbers at the school had recovered a little; it was still extremely small, but Vicesimus Knox had put it on the map. In 1812 the Governors appointed his younger son Thomas as his successor.

'Sir Sidney Smith on the Walls of Acre.' Sir Sidney Smith, who left school at an early age to join the Navy, was a loyal OT. Napoleon regarded him as one of his most formidable opponents. He also thought he was quite mad.

A small watercolour of Thomas Knox, artist unknown, early nineteenth century. This portrait, and that of Vicesimus Knox on page 21, were recently discovered in Australia and sold to the school. We know that one of Thomas Knox's sons emigrated to Australia.

1812 was a memorable year, and it is a good moment to take stock. Britain was about to enter on a period of military success followed by the economic depression that so often follows a great war. The coming of the railways and industrial growth were still some years away. The town of Tonbridge had prospered through the war and was ideally placed to take advantage of any economic benefits to come, but, before that, Tonbridge's only bank failed, and its downfall brought severe hardship to two of Tonbridge's wealthiest families – the Woodgates of Summerhill and the Childrens of Ferox Hall.

The school was still some years away from the changes which were to increase its numbers out of recognition, but, unlike many schools of the time, it had had at least 50 years of civilized headmastership. There is no evidence of the bullying and misery which pervaded most boarding schools at the time. The assumption must be that Towers and the Knoxes probably made life for boarders as bearable as possible within the tight financial restraints which still prevailed. The Governors in London had fulfilled their obligations for 250 years, but had provided no major buildings apart from Cawthorn's Library.

We do not, sadly, know many details about the school at this time. We know that boys still entered the school at only eight years of age and that there was little departure from a rigid and tedious classical curriculum. This certainly deterred most of the local tradesmen from sending their sons to the school, but there is no evidence of unhappiness, and the fact that a French general bothered to make the hazardous journey to Tonbridge to look up his old Headmaster in the middle of a war must tell us something.

When Thomas Knox became Headmaster in 1812, it might have been the beginning of a new era, but it was not. It was the last stage of an old one. The period was to be played out against a background of economic and political change, but the most significant change at Tonbridge was to be the increasing importance of cricket. To some Tonbridgians over the next 180 years cricket, or even the mention of it, was to be distasteful: to many others, Tonbridge and cricket have become synonymous.

Apart from the references in Clemence Dane's song to football and cricket, no mention of sport at the school survives up to this date, apart from a poem by Thomas Knox himself, written while still a boy at the school. It is called 'The Tonbridge School Boy' and it mentions cricket. Cricket certainly figures frequently in local newspapers from 1770 onwards, and Thomas Knox was a keen supporter of the game.

Eton first played Westminster in 1796, but Tonbridge's first school match, against Brighton, did not take place until 1856. Some commentators believe that Dickens's description of a cricket match in *Pickwick Papers* is based on an account he read of a match played at Tonbridge School in 1832. Accounts do exist of an annual match at the school between the local bachelors and the local married men, but these matches were for adults. Cricket clubs were flourishing and had many keen female supporters, one of whom was Frances Woodgate, who became Thomas Knox's wife.

Tonbridge's first cricket blue was J. Abercrombie for Cambridge in 1839. Presumably he played serious cricket while at school 1828–34. In the 1839 Varsity match, he was absent in the first innings, possibly because he was also in the Cambridge boat, and made nought in the second.

Two events, 40 years apart, which were to affect Thomas Knox's reign, predated it and had no connection with cricket. In 1765 a small boy, barely eight years old, arrived at the school from the remote West Indian island of St Kitts, and in 1806 the Duke of Bedford's lease on Sir Andrew Judde's sheepfields in St Pancras expired. Different as they at first seem, these two events were to combine to put the school on a totally new footing.

The small boy was Anthony Hart, the youngest of three brothers. He was at the school from 1765 to 1775. He became a barrister and the most celebrated advocate at the Chancery bar. He was first appointed Vice-Chancellor of England and then Chancellor of Ireland. He was at the height of his powers when the school became involved yet again in legal action over the true meaning of Sir Andrew Judde's will. Sir Anthony Hart agreed to represent the school in the long case which followed. The complexities of this case would drive most readers to abandon this book, but it is crucial to the story of the school's development, and a nutshell account must be attempted.

In 1807 London was expanding rapidly, especially to the north, as the names Regent Street and Regent's Park show. The great builder of the time, James Burton, who lived near Tonbridge, took building leases on the Judde lands opposite where St Pancras station now stands. He built several streets, like Judd Street, which can still be seen. Naturally the annual income from this land increased – on this occasion from a few pounds to £4,000 a year. As this sum was several times the annual income of the school, various parties claimed it. The townspeople claimed it in order to obtain free education for their sons. The Headmaster claimed it to increase the salaries of himself and his Usher – their salaries had hardly doubled in 250 years! The Skinners' Company claimed it because they said that any excess, after the school's expenses had been paid, belonged to them. To be fair to the Skinners, they had frequently subsidized the school and fought legal cases on its behalf out of their own funds. This strange triangular conflict between friends might possibly have been settled out of court, but for government interference.

From 1812 onwards, in the period leading up to the Great Reform Act, there was a great deal of parliamentary activity, as a reforming Parliament sought to concern itself with all aspects of the nation's life. Two areas of its concern were education and charities. In 1818 a commission was set up to investigate educational charities, and when the Commissioners came to Tonbridge, they carried out a full and lengthy cross-questioning of the Headmaster and of the Clerk to the Skinners' Company, of which complete records exist. Thomas Knox gave a full account of the history of the school and the Clerk gave a detailed report of the money the Governors had spent on the school. Inevitably the question of who was entitled to the new income was raised, and the Commissioners wisely suggested that a court decision would be the best answer.

So, in 1819, a long Chancery case began. The terms of Andrew Judde's will, Fisher's will, Judde's deed of gift, Judde's statutes and the two Elizabethan Acts of Parliament confirming them, were discussed at great length. Anthony Hart, by then an old man, put the school's case to such good effect that the school won a complete victory. The court decided that the school was to reap the full benefit of Judde's bequest and all the extra income. From this point on the school's finances were transformed.

Over the next few years a new scheme for the school was prepared and approved by the Lord Chancellor. It was to take the school into a new age, though it was to be superseded by another new scheme 50 years later. The new scheme of 1825, later amended by the Governors in 1844, covered several pages and 54 sections, dealing with everything from salaries to working hours.

The Headmaster's salary was raised from its 1759 level of £62 a year to £500 a year and the Usher's from £40 to £200. The Usher was to be called the Second Master and provided with a separate house.

Various wordy clauses were inserted to demand propriety and sobriety from them both, together with strange warnings about impotence and about not going off with school property when they left. Holiday times and lesson times were fixed, and the Headmaster given the right to award twelve extra days a year on special occasions. One of these occasions was Guy Fawkes Day, and the building and lighting of the bonfire behind the school became one of the big events of the year for the school and the town.

The boys were to be formed into two classes – foundationers and non-foundationers. Sixteen leaving exhibitions to Oxford and Cambridge were to be founded – four exhibitions lasting four years each. Foundationers were to be given priority in the award of these exhibitions. This last clause was to create immense problems and controversy for the next 50 years, almost as if, having solved one major legal problem, the school had a masochistic desire to saddle itself with another, which would one day involve Mr Gladstone.

These statutes can be read in full in Rivington: unfortunately they seem dry and irrelevant now, which is why Rivington, a far more scholarly and worthy book than this, is rarely read.

The visible results of the new scheme are more easily understood. The old school building was far too small and visibly deteriorating. The Governors agreed to some major rebuilding. A new wing for the junior school was built at the north end, and Cawthorn's Library at the south end was extended upwards to match the new wing in height and appearance. A new dining-room was built at the back, with dormitories overhead. The Georgian building on the High Street, to the north of the new junior school, was purchased as a boarding-house for the Second Master, the Revd. Thomas Brown, and renamed Judde House. The old trees and wall in front of the school were replaced by an iron railing.

'The Cricket Match at Tonbridge School, 1851', by C. T. Dodd sen. Charles Tattershall Dodd was Drawing Master 1834–78. 'The Cricket Match at Tonbridge School' – an oil-painting – is probably his best known oil-painting, though his other paintings of Tonbridge and Tunbridge Wells, where he lived, were very popular in his day. The final version of the picture showed a certain amount of artistic licence – particularly the positioning of the Headmaster, the Revd. J. I. Welldon, and the Second Master, the Revd. E. I. Welldon, well within the boundary.

'The Cricket Match at Tonbridge School', by C. T. Dodd Sen., 1851. The preliminary sketch, a water-colour, which hangs in the school Library.

'Tonbridge School', by C. T. Dodd sen., 1845. There are at least three versions of this painting. In Dodd's first version one of the boys was carrying a hoop, and this upset the boys and OTs who said that Tonbridge boys did not play with hoops. Marbles possibly, or hop-scotch, but not hoops. So Dodd re painted it with the hoop painted out.

The Old Upper School till 1864. Until the building of the Lower School in 1826, all classes were taught in this one room.

The financial difficulties of the Children family at Ferox Hall meant that Ferox Hall, an old Tudor building directly opposite the Headmaster's, was on the market, and the Governors, foreseeing a future need to expand, sent their surveyor to look at it. He reported that it would need vast expenditure and was not worth buying. It was decided to expand in the other direction – on to Martin's land behind the school. Judde's original site consisted of little more than the main buildings fronting the High Street and a small playing-area at the back of the school. Beyond this stretched farmland belonging to a farmer called Martin.

In 1826 the Governors purchased the field which now contains the main 1st XI cricket ground and the patches of ground to the north and south of it, later called the Upper and Lower Hundreds. These names, which have become entrenched, were at some time taken from the numbers on the various games organized by the boys, just as the 1st XI ground was called the 'Head Eleven' or 'Head Club'. Later, 'Head Eleven' was shortened to 'the Head', the confusing name by which it is still known. By similar schoolboy logic the main rugger ground has always been called the 'Fifty'. When Somervell's history was published in 1947, with Tattershall Dodd's famous 1851 oil-painting of 'Cricket on the Head' as its frontispiece, the printers of the first edition refused to believe it was called 'the Head' and printed it as *Cricket on the Mead*. The name has always confused the uninitiated, but the purchase of this land from Mr Martin was one of the most important moves ever made by the Governors. The new limits to the school property were marked by iron 'scratching-posts' bearing the date

The Scratching-Posts, as they are now called, were erected to mark the boundaries of the school grounds in 1826. Several of them still survive, but it is doubtful if they are in their original positions.

1826, and some of these scratching-posts can still be seen at the bottom of the Avenue, though they are not in their original position.

In 1838 Thomas Knox took the momentous decision to level the Head and use earth and labour from the new railway workings. The labourers were lodged near the school, and were involved in frequent fights with the boys, as described in full in an Old Boy's letter in Rivington. The Head, described by a famous cricketing journalist as one of the two flattest pitches in the South, immediately became the focal point of the school. Not many schools have the benefit of a beautiful, almost sacred, piece of ground right at the heart of the school. I recently found a lady visitor staring at it. 'Can I help you?' I asked. She smiled: 'I've lived all over the world,' she replied, 'and this is the most beautiful spot on earth. I always come back to it, and that's my grandson out there playing on it.' When she went on to add that she hoped in the next life to come back as a housemaster's wife, I decided she must be dotty, but it was a nice compliment.

Unfortunately there are a few misguided people – mainly scientists – who do not view the Head in the same light. It was rumoured recently that the annual cost of fertilizing it exceeds the allowance of several departments. Tonbridge's buildings, to a visitor, may not at first sight seem all that impressive; yet, seen across the Head on a summer evening, reflecting the waning sun, they assume a dreamy, almost surrealist beauty. Knox's foresight is staggering. He not only bought a cricket field – he created a masterpiece. The original plaque commemorating this event was lost, but a replica can be seen in the present pavilion:

> Hanc aream aequandam curavit Thomas Knox S.T.P. huius scholae magister
> AD 1838

Yet, in spite of the enlarged buildings and grounds the school still did not prosper. As Somervell says, 'The banquet was prepared, but the guests did not arrive.' The failure of the Tonbridge Bank had had a disastrous effect on the town and bankrupted some of the wealthy families who sent their sons to the school. What is more, Thomas Knox had inherited some of his father's radical spirit and loved politics. Elections in Tonbridge frequently led to riots in the High Street, as can be seen in the Tattershall Dodd brothers' paintings. Thomas Knox could not resist making speeches which offended those on whom the school depended for its custom. Numbers declined, and it needed a shrewder Headmaster to take advantage of the school's new-found wealth. Knox was clearly a man of the early and not the middle nineteenth century. There are some marvellous letters from Old Boys about him in Rivington. Three brief extracts are given below:

> We walked up with my father to see Dr Knox . . . we found him in his garden and he took us over the school and grounds. Well do I remember his fine and portly figure, his shaggy eyebrows and bright eye, and on my father saying his boys had brought their bats, the doctor remarked, 'Yes, quite right, quite right: I never knew a boy worth anything who was not fond of cricket.'

Punishment was almost always corporal. The unheard of punishment of writing out 500 lines of Homer was once given by the doctor who caught a boy *flagrante delicto*, riding his favorite heifer round the cricket field.

There was the doctor on horseback, taking a hearty interest in the game, there were the townspeople sitting on the slopes, sucking their pipes and drinking beer and cider. . . . Then at one o'clock the two elevens and the whole school used to adjourn to the dining hall and dine together. It was one of the merriest days of the year, and no one apparently enjoyed it more than the doctor himself, who not infrequently would sing them 'The Brave Old Oak' or 'The Old English Gentleman'.

Thomas Knox died in the parish church near the end of the summer term of 1843, while preparing to preach. He was a popular man in the town, if not the intellectual equal of his father. The Knoxes had reigned for 71 years.

THE TWO WELLDONS

The celebrity of our school depends not a little on our capabilities as cricketers.

The Tonbridgian: *Editorial, 1859*

J. I. Welldon by T. Blake Wirgman.

The Governors moved fast to find Thomas Knox's successor, and the new Headmaster took up his post in September 1843. The man they chose was the Revd. James Ind Welldon. Born in 1811, he went to school in Norfolk and then to St John's College, Cambridge, where he obtained a first in Classics and Mathematics. For seven years he was Second Master at Shrewsbury, one of the most important schools in the country, where he served under two famous headmasters, Butler and Kennedy.

Welldon's appointment opens a completely new chapter from the historian's point of view, because the amount of written material available suddenly increases a hundredfold. There are several reasons for this: first the Governors' records of the school were separated from their other records and kept in a special minute-book. Secondly, Welldon kept his own records, which have survived, and which, for want of a better word, I shall refer to as his 'Yearbook'. Next, Rivington, who published the first edition of his *History of Tonbridge School* in 1869, was a pupil of Welldon's, and the later editions of Rivington contain several letters from OTs describing Welldon and the school in his time. They also contain some reminiscences which Welldon dictated just before his death. Finally, *The Tonbridgian* first appeared in 1858, and gives us an invaluable record of school activities from then on.

Knox's death not only marked the end of the Knox dynasty, but it came at a time when England was about to be transformed by the Industrial Revolution, with its effect on the middle classes in the South-East. In 1842 there had been two other significant events. Thomas Arnold of Rugby had died suddenly, having completed his work of making boarding schools popular with the middle class as well as the gentry; and the South-Eastern Railway had finally opened its line from London to Tonbridge, via Redhill.

When Welldon came to Tonbridge, the school badly needed a new

broom, who would take advantage of these new opportunities. Numbers

broom, who would take advantage of these new opportunities. Numbers
had dropped to 43 and Welldon was unhappy both with the state of the
boys and of the buildings. He was not very impressed with his predecessor.
He said that Thomas Knox always came into school late, and that on the
clock which hung at one end of the schoolroom (*see* p.27) the boys had
written opposite the figure eleven 'Nox Venit'. He was appalled at the state
of the dormitories, which had such low ceilings that he banged his head.

To start with, the boys found Welldon severe and forbidding, and it was
felt that he tried too hard to turn Tonbridge into a copy of Shrewsbury,
but the boys' opinion of him soon softened, and tributes to him and
anecdotes about him abound. Parents obviously approved of him because
within two years numbers rose from 43 to 139. By the middle of his reign,
a feeling of affection for the school among the Old Boys was established,
which had not existed before.

Welldon's 'Yearbook' is an extraordinary book: it is extremely heavy. It

The first railway station, 1842–68, here shown in a drawing by Geo. E. Mackley, was on the other side of the railway bridge. It was smaller and more open than the present one. It was customary for the citizens of Tonbridge to put on their best clothes and gather on the platform to greet very important people, such as royalty, who had landed at Dover and were on their way to London. It was the duty of the Headmaster's wife to arrange the seating plan at the station. The train would stop, the visiting royalty would alight and be introduced to the local dignitaries. Stories abound of these occasions, though their sources are hard to trace. On one occasion they were all sitting there waiting for the Sultan of Turkey and the train went straight through without stopping. On another occasion the train did stop and the aides of the visiting Nabob or Emperor seized a pretty Tonbridge girl and dragged her into a carriage. Once all the locals had their watches and purses stolen by two pickpockets. This episode, which had a happy ending, is described in Neve's Tonbridge of Yesteryear.

'Tonbridge School' by C. T. Dodd sen., 1845. This is the version with a boy carrying a hoop which caused the controversy (see plate facing page 27).

Revd. E. I. Welldon, Second Master.

'The Second Master's Residence', artist and date unknown. This Georgian building, now known as Old Judde, was originally a private house and was purchased as the Second Master's house and the second boarding-house in 1826. The name Judde House was not used until the 1850s.

has over 400 large pages, some of which contain just one letter, but many have several documents pasted on them. In the days before secretaries and filing systems, it acted as a mobile filing cabinet. In it he pasted all the letters he received on important issues as well as copies of the letters he sent out. The latter are almost without exception illegible. If anybody could ever read it, it would be worth publishing for its own sake. I have done my best to decipher it. He also left behind his 'Punishment Book' which should be fascinating, but the interesting bits are illegible.

In his early years, Welldon managed to upset parents and, one suspects, Governors, and some of the earliest entries in the 'Yearbook' concern these disputes. He believed in use of the cane, but only as a last resort, and he replaced caning mainly with impositions. However, in June 1844, he caned the Curate's nine-year-old son hard enough to make the Curate complain to the Governors.

> This youth was punished by the Master, by means of a rod upon his naked person, with such severity as to stain his linen considerably with blood.

The Governors demanded an explanation, and Welldon replied that he used only the same punishment methods as used at Eton. The boy was punished for being the ringleader of a group of boys who had grossly insulted the Second Master by hissing at him. In any case the boy could not have been badly hurt as he saw him down town later that afternoon. The Governors decided not to interfere.

Shortly after, he expelled a boy who had been seen coming out of a house of ill-repute. The boy claimed that he had mistaken it for the house of a day boy. The boy's guardian protested that his ward did not have enough pocket-money for such extra-curricular activity. On this occasion the Governors rebuked Welldon for expelling a boy without informing them or the guardian in advance.

In 1844 Welldon appointed his younger brother, the Revd. Edward Ind Welldon to the staff, and the two brothers were to form a partnership lasting over 30 years. Edward, or Teddy as he was known, was a stern though popular schoolmaster who was to devote the rest of his life to the school. In Tattershall Dodd's famous picture you can see them standing together watching the cricket. Dodd, for some reason has them standing well inside the boundary. For 30 years the two Welldons were Tonbridge School.

Welldon bombarded the Governors with requests for money to be spent on repairs and extra accommodation, but he met with polite and constant refusals. There was no money available in the Foundation, he was politely informed by the Clerk, Mr Kensit, whose reign at Skinners' Hall lasted even longer than Welldon's at Tonbridge, and who seemed to treat the Headmaster's letters with polite forbearance.

Other changes Welldon was able to implement. In 1845 the first printed exams were introduced, and Maths was put in the charge of a separate master – the first major departure from the old Classical curriculum for 300 years. What concerned Welldon most in these early years, however, was the lack of a chapel. Several schools had chapels, and it is perhaps surprising that Judde had not included one in his original plans. Like Arnold, Welldon thought that chapel should be the centre of school life, a place where boys could be taught the difference between right and wrong. In vain he applied for funds to the Governors. They refused, saying that they did not wish to contravene the Founder's statutes with their commitment to the parish church; the real reason was probably that there was no money available. In 1848 Welldon decided to raise the money for a new chapel himself by public appeal, and he had a leaflet printed and circulated. The first the Governors knew of the scheme was when they received the leaflet. They were naturally upset and told him to abandon the project.

From this time copies survive of the Latin prayers in use at the school: two of these Latin prayers, which were then used morning, midday and evening, are now only said once a year at the Skinners' Day service. The school motto too dates from this time. Welldon was hanging a shield with the school arms on his study wall, when he realized the school had no motto. He decided it should be – 'Deus dat Incrementum', which it has been ever since. Perhaps he was thinking about his new chapel.

In 1851 there was a serious fire in the roof of the Lower School, which workmen were converting into a classroom and extra studies. They had lit a fire to melt their glue and failed to put it out. At two in the morning the fire erupted and set the roof alight. Fortunately, a young man studying in his bedroom opposite the school saw the fire and raised the alarm in time for it to be put out with water brought from a nearby pond.

In 1853 the school celebrated its tercentenary. A large number of Old Boys and friends of the school attended, and the Archbishop of Canterbury, Dr Sumner, preached at the service in the parish church. Welldon was presented by the boys with a silver vase and a plaster model of the school as it was in 1853, which is still to be seen in the library. Dr Sumner was the last Archbishop to wear a wig, and many years later

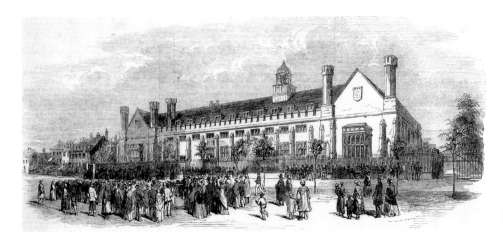

'The Tonbridge School Tercentenary Celebrations', 1853. Artist unknown. Published originally in the Illustrated London News.

one OT writing about his confirmation by Sumner said that he was so amazed by the wig that he could not remember anything else about the service. The OT went on to become a clergyman.

In 1853 the first concert was held and was to become an annual event of great popularity with the school and town. It was shortly to replace the bonfire as the big annual event of the winter. In 1858 the bonfire was banned because of the large number of accidents, in particular the death of a boy who contracted pneumonia while preparing it.

Welldon's relations with the town were not always easy. In 1854 a resident of the town insisted on taking three Tonbridge schoolboys to court for throwing snowballs at him in the street. The Tonbridge magistrates dismissed the case and rebuked the complainant, pointing out that it was Dr Welldon's duty to punish the boys, which he had done. The same year some local citizens protested at the idea of Teddy Welldon starting his own prep school and wrote to the Governors complaining of the way the school was being run. A large majority of day-boy parents, however, wrote to Welldon offering him their support.

A year later a much more serious problem arose, when another day-boy parent, the Revd. Robert Shepherd, brought a case on behalf of his son against two boarders who had struck the day boy with a cane for cutting fagging. Fagging in those days mainly consisted of small boys having to take turns in fielding and fetching cricket balls and footballs for the seniors. Many day boys were able to avoid the task by producing 'leave off' certificates, signed by their parents on medical grounds. There was considerable feeling among the boarders that day boys did not play their full part in school activities, particularly sport. Welldon was inclined to back the boarders, particularly those in School House. After the Tonbridge magistrates had dismissed the case, Shepherd took it to a higher court, claiming that Welldon discriminated against day boys, and at Westminster Hall the judge found the boarders guilty, fined them £5 each, but refused to grant costs either way. It was a long-drawn-out episode, and once again the majority of day-boy parents wrote to Welldon offering him their support, saying they had no complaint about the way he treated their sons.

In 1855 Thomas Brown retired and died soon afterwards. Teddy Welldon was appointed Second Master and moved into Brown's house. This house, of 40 boarders, Judde House, was first known as Brown's and then as E. Welldon's or Teddy's, and is now known as Old Judde.

In 1858 the Governors sanctioned the erection of three wooden class-rooms by the side of the playground, one of which became the VIth-form class-room. These huts were hot in summer and cold and draughty in winter, but they were to serve for 43 years. In 1859 the Governors finally gave Welldon permission to raise money for the erection of a chapel between the main school building and Judde House. Events moved rapidly; the foundation stone was laid in May 1859, and the chapel opened by the Archbishop in October. The cost of £2,500 was raised by an appeal to which the Governors contributed privately. They had finally conceded that the Founder's wishes could be met by the boys' attending the church just once on Sundays. Henceforward they would attend the school chapel on weekdays and once on Sundays. The chapel was built to seat only 200, and within 30 years it was too small for its purpose.

In 1858 two other events happened of great significance. It was the year in which the first cricket 1st XI and the football XI were officially recorded, and it was also the year in which *The Tonbridgian* made its first appearance. *The Tonbridgian* was far from being the first school magazine, but it claims to be the oldest school magazine with an unbroken sequence – a claim confirmed in a letter to the *Sunday Times* in May 1927 by an anonymous correspondent, who listed the starting dates of all the early school magazines and whose findings were not questioned.

The first edition appeared on 1 June 1858, since when it has not missed an issue. The school library contains at least one complete set. For many years there were ten issues a year, costing sixpence an issue, a price which did not rise for 30 years. Many other school magazines failed for financial reasons, and *The Tonbridgian* nearly did, but in 1863 Welldon was persuaded to make it compulsory for boarders to buy it, which led to further resentment against the day boys. For the next 100 years it made a profit which was given to a special fund to subsidize various school activities. At first the top five boys in the VIth form were editors, and it was very much a magazine by boys for boys. Virtually uncensored, it provided a panorama of school life. Somervell admits that he based much of his book on it, and so do I. Debates, concerts, lectures, match reports, complaints, requests for more contributions pour from its pages. It is particularly valuable in dating the sporting events which were, from 1858 onward, to play such a major role in the life of the school.

We know that cricket had started much earlier in the century, if not before. If you read Dickens, you will know that it was a very popular sport both with adults and children. The first time the school played the Old Boys with an 'unstrengthened' side was in 1846. The first school match was against Brighton College in 1856. In 1858 colours were introduced and in 1860 the cricket pavilion was built, again by appeal.

In 1861 a set of rules of the Tonbridge School Cricket Club was issued covering 43 articles and 15 pages. Rules were very rigid. The Club was divided into a Head Eleven of 26, who were to be elected annually and a Second, Third, Fourth and Fifth Club, each with a 'patronus' from a higher club. Soon matches were being played down as far as 6th XI level. One strange result of this system was that for a time the XI batted in order of their election, not their batting ability. (I once read an account, which I can no longer find, that at one time they batted in order of size!)

Each club was to have its own ground and wear a white shirt with a different-coloured cap and belt – the 1st XI's white shirts had a blue stripe down the front, the Second Club Upper XI wore a red cap, trimmed with white. There were playing members who had to play and could use the school kit, and ordinary members who did not have to play, and could not

The first page in the earliest score-book in the school library. Early score-books were very like modern ones. Scores in the early days, as in this match against Brighton in 1859, were consistently low.

use the school kit if they did. J. Gaythorne Hardy, in his book on public schools, says Tonbridge was the first school to introduce colours.

The captain in 1858 was H. St J. Reade who went on to captain Oxford and become Headmaster of Oundle. *The Tonbridgian* gives the 1st XI score-cards in full from 1858 onwards. The first match listed is against Mr Fleming's pupils. Mr Fleming, also known as Le Fleming, ran a school for older boys – a kid of crammer – in Eton House, now known as Smythe House, and his field adjoined the Head.

The oldest surviving score-book is for 1859. Score-books and score-cards of those days are almost like modern ones, except for a few details, such as 'thrown out' as well as 'run out', and the first 'stumped' is not recorded until 1871. Possibly the wicket-keeper was merely a long-stop, because one Tonbridge family boasted that all its six sons were 1st XI long-stops in turn. There was a large number of wides, and on the whole scores were low. Whether matches were one or two innings seems to have been an *ad hoc* decision made as the match developed. Cricket experts could no doubt answer these questions in their sleep. By 1861 the cricket XI had 20 matches a year, though Brighton remained the only school match for some years. In 1859 *The Tonbridgian* was moved to claim that Tonbridge's reputation as a school depended mainly on its cricket (see above). This is a rather arrogant claim, as we only played Brighton, who were looked down on for being a private school and arriving on the day of the match instead of the night before. The following plea for better fixtures reflects the school's desire to be more widely accepted.

> We only play one school match, and that with a private school. . . . And the plan I have to propose is that for the future we play our equals and not our inferiors. Sir, there is Winchester School, there is St Paul's School, there is Charter House School (Letter to the Editor of *The Tonbridgian*, 1863).

Football developed from a motley assortment of playground rough-houses. Much has been written about the roughness of the original Tonbridge game, and the school found it difficult to find opponents because it was so tough. By 1858 protests against football fagging and the habit of standing all the small boys in goal led to the creation of lower games, and in 1859 the boys were divided into a 30, a 50 and an 80. Even 40 a side cannot have been much fun for the eight-year-olds. In 1864 football fagging was abolished. From 1858 football became more civilized, and in 1870 the Rugby code was adopted rather than Association Football because it involved more boys. By 1872 two OTs, Luscombe and Body, were playing for England: Luscombe captained England twice and became Vice-President of the RFU.

From 1846, the names of Head Boys are listed in the school register. Reade was Head Boy in 1857–8 and was regarded by Welldon as the best one he had, saying that he helped him tackle the drinking problem which was prevalent. Welldon introduced the system of monitors, with distinctive clothing, and from then on many more activities, especially the

games clubs, were controlled by boys. A boat club was started in 1860 and did not last long, but the athletic sports became a popular event. They were held on the Head, reported in great detail by *The Tonbridgian* and supported fervently by the local ladies, who started presenting prizes, and soon *The Tonbridgian* was complaining of a surfeit of prizes. Some of the prizes were open to outsiders, and that led to complaints about professional 'pot-hunters'. Paperchasing had been popular (or unpopular, *see* page 45) for many years, but one day the hares took the hounds as far as Tunbridge Wells and Speldhurst and back, and the juniors were still staggering in after midnight, after which junior boys were banned from taking part in the senior paperchase.

The only other sports were swimming in the doubtful waters of the Medway below the town; gymnastics, held in a broken-down open shed containing almost no equipment; and fives, played both with a bat or with hands, in a variety of courts. Two of the bat fives courts can be seen in Dodd's picture, looking rather like a cricket screen. Apparently they were the only ones in the world. There were frequent requests for a bathing-shed and a cleaner bathing area away from the effluents of the Tonbridge factories. The first swimming sports were held in 1859. There was a popular pastime called 'stumper' or stump cricket, a kind of rounders and a 'Giant's Leap'.

Numbers increased steadily after the opening of the new chapel, and the clergy started to send their sons to the school. The first staff picture of 1863 shows a staff of eleven, including E. H. Goggs who was to stay at the school for 34 years: in 1863 Mr Hayden was appointed organist and choirmaster. Most of the musical activities were concentrated on singing, at which Goggs excelled, and the annual concert. Welldon disliked drama, saying that the only plays should be in Greek, and there is no mention of drama until 1870.

In 1859 a small group of OTs – A. Knox, the son of Thomas Knox, A. de Fonblanque and Tom Nottidge – met at the OT cricket match and

Above left. *Old Boys XI, 1863. One of the OTs shown is A. Knox, son of Dr T. Knox, the previous headmaster.*

Above. *Rugger XIII, 1865–6. This is the earliest rugger photo, and the XIII includes F. Luscombe who went on to captain England and become Vice-President of the RFU.*

decided to organize an OT Dinner. In 1860, the first dinner, apart from the one in 1744, was held at The Ship at Greenwich, and the OT Dinner has been held ever since apart from a few early years and the war years.

The school's rising fortunes date back to the Court decision of 1820, and in 1862 the gods were to look kindly on the school once more. After years of being denied funds for development, Welldon was suddenly asked by the Governors what he would do with a large sum of money. The Midland Railway Company needed part of the Sandhills estate for its new goods-yard next to St Pancras Station. An Act of Parliament empowered it to purchase the land compulsorily. The sums of money were out of all proportion to anything the Foundation had received before, and one can only wonder what Sir Andrew Judde, up in Heaven, thought about it all.

'And first you are to remember your Founder, Sir Andrew Judde, Knight,' says the beautiful bidding prayer used on Skinners' Day, written at about this time. Few schools have ever had this type of good fortune or such a far-seeing Founder.

Welldon proposed the pulling down of the old school and the building of a new one. The old building was in a bad state, and the local health inspector admitted that he would have condemned the School House dormitories as unfit for human habitation if his own son had not been sleeping in them at the time.

The foundation stone was laid in May 1863 by the Master of the Skinners' Company, who apologized for doing so instead of the Prince of Wales, but said that the Skinners could not afford the latter. The new foundation stone contained a metal canister holding documents and photos

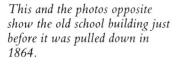

This and the photos opposite show the old school building just before it was pulled down in 1864.

of the time, including that of Goggs, as he was proud to boast for the rest of his life.

The new building, set back about 60 yards from the old building, was open for use by the beginning of the summer term a year later. The old building was immediately pulled down, apart from part of the Headmaster's house which was preserved and joined to the new building by the ugliest piece of masonry in Tonbridge. Some subscribers to *The Tonbridgian* regretted the passing of their old haunts and even disapproved of the new cubicles, always called 'cubies', built upstairs for the School House boys. The new building was higher than the old one, and the School House boys started to climb out on to the parapet, so that Welldon had to have bars installed to stop them killing themselves. The main feature of the new building was a large hall, now known as Old Big School.

In 1867 the Revd. J. R. Little opened Park House as a boarding-house for 20 boys. It was the first House outside the school grounds and was privately owned. In 1869 Welldon drove to Uppingham with Mitchinson, the Headmaster of King's Canterbury, to attend the conference from which the Headmasters' Conference was to evolve. The meeting was chaired and dominated by Thring of Uppingham, but the records show that Welldon made a major contribution to the discussions. His time at Tonbridge was drawing to a close, and his latter years must have been made more anxious by an endless dispute between the Governors and the Government. This problem needs a chapter of its own, but it is very tedious and discussed in full in Rivington. Even *The Tonbridgian* found little humorous to say about it. Briefly this is what is was about.

In 1858 the Government set up the Endowed Schools Commission to investigate the 'big nine' – Eton, Winchester and Co. As a result, the governing bodies of these schools were radically altered. In 1864 the powers of the Commission were widened, and Tonbridge was examined. Welldon and the Governors were questioned and certain drastic proposals put forward by the Commission in 1867, including reducing the Skinners'

Below left. A view of the back of the old school before it was pulled down in 1864.

Below. The new school buildings were built in 1864, about 60 yards behind the old building, where school continued as usual until the new building was complete. This is a rare photo of work progressing on the new building.

representation on the governing body to a half. The Governors were alarmed by these proposals and put forward a scheme of their own. The argument raged for the rest of Welldon's time and deterred the Governors from spending any more money on the school.

Welldon had attempted to widen the curriculum, but he was at heart a confirmed classicist, and, apart from appointing H. Hilary to teach Maths, he had failed to meet the challenge of the new age. In 1875 he announced his resignation and retired to the parish of Kennington near Ashford, where he was to spend 20 very active years ministering to his parishioners. He had been made an Honorary Canon of Canterbury in 1873.

Somervell reckons that he was the greatest Headmaster Tonbridge had had. Hoole is more reserved on the subject, pointing out some of his weaknesses, particularly his failure to introduce Science subjects. He was also slow in recognizing the value of music and drama to a boy's education, but he was not alone in this. He probably could have done more to improve the status of day boys. Nevertheless, Tonbridge was a very different school when Welldon left: he lacked the dynamism of some of his contemporaries, like Thring, and he was not flamboyant, but he was a sound administrator, and his Old Boys thought the world of him.

When he left there were 239 boys in the school. It is certain that they all regretted his going and told stories about him for years afterwards. He received several gifts from the boys, the OTs and residents of the town as well as cheques for over a thousand pounds – a quite staggering sum in modern terms. A man of simple tastes who enjoyed walking and riding and abhorred smoking, who was devoted to his 'lads', and believed in honesty and self-reliance, he was dedicated to Tonbridge. The latest Welldon – the fifth generation – has just left the school.

Common Room photo – 1875. J. H. Stubbs, W. G. Williams, Revd. C. Walters, H. Hilary, Revd. J. Langhorne, W. E. McGill, E. H. Goggs, Revd. J. I. Welldon, Revd. E. I. Welldon, Revd. J. R. Little.

6

T. B. ROWE

It seems a great pity that a Football Match with Dulwich hardly ever passes without a dispute of some kind.

The Tonbridgian: *Editorial, 1881*

When the Governors appointed the Revd. T. B. Rowe to succeed Dr Welldon in 1876, they must have thought they had made a shrewd choice. Rowe had been a housemaster at Uppingham for 15 years, and Uppingham was then at the height of its fame under Edward Thring who had been a leading light in the formation of the Headmasters' Conference in 1869. Thring had introduced many changes at Uppingham which made the school a leader among public schools. Thring had met some opposition there, but Rowe had been his right-hand man and greatest supporter.

Now, at the age of 42, Rowe was faced at Tonbridge with the task of following Dr Welldon, an extremely popular Headmaster, already almost a legend, with sons at the school and still living not far away. Rowe was to find Welldon a difficult act to follow.

Born in 1833, Theophilus Barton Rowe was educated at Durham Cathedral School and St John's College, Cambridge where he obtained a 1st in Classics and Maths. In 1861 Thring invited him to Uppingham, where he was in charge of the Lower VIth and a housemaster.

T. B. Rowe, by G. P. Jacomb Hood (OT).

When he came to Tonbridge in 1876 he faced formidable difficulties:

1. The school had just ended a long, benevolent and relatively happy reign under J. I. Welldon.

2. E. I. Welldon was still Second Master.

3. The long-awaited 'New Scheme' had still not been finalized.

4. The staff and the school were fed up with all the uncertainty about the New Scheme.

5. The Governors still did not know if they were going to remain as sole governors under the New Scheme.

6. To meet the demands of whatever new scheme was adopted, more staff and more buildings would be needed to meet the wider curriculum envisaged, but the Governors were not prepared to spend money on a school which might soon be taken away from them.

7. The townspeople were angry with the school, the Governors and the Charity Commissioners for a variety of reasons, and pamphlets were flying in all directions.

Poor Rowe! Perhaps he should have taken the first train back to Uppingham! The Governors misled him by telling him that the New Scheme would definitely come into force in 1876. They were far too optimistic – or pessimistic – it did not come into effect until 1 January 1881. In the circumstances Rowe did his best to plan the future of the school round what he thought the New Scheme would involve, and his headmastership divides into two parts – the periods before and after the implementation of the New Scheme.

Now, with hindsight, we can assess Rowe's success or lack of it. Rivington states the facts of his case and gives him quite a good press, though implying that he was not the man his predecessor was. Somervell, who idolized Welldon, treats him rather dismissively.

> Mr Rowe was in many respects an enlightened man, more up to date in his ideas than Dr Welldon perhaps. But he was not nearly so successful a headmaster. Though a fine scholar, an inspiring teacher and an amiable character, he was afflicted with an intellectual honesty which impelled him to say exactly what he thought about people and things at all times, and he sometimes gave utterance to his real thoughts on occasions when more worldly guile would have dictated reticence.

An honest Headmaster – and Somervell does not approve of him! To be fair, however, he goes on to admit that Rowe gave the school a sharp intellectual stimulus. I shall list Rowe's achievements and let the reader judge for himself, but I cannot help mentioning a bizarre sequel to this remark of Somervell's.

Rowe's first wife died in 1887 and he remarried late in life. By his second wife he had two daughters. In 1949 his daughters wrote to the then Headmaster, Lawrence Waddy, asking very politely if any future edition of a school history could give their father a kinder review. They included copies of various tributes to their father paid at the time of his death in 1905. In 1976, a hundred years after his appointment, further correspondence on this subject took place between one of his daughters and the Headmaster, Christopher Everett. I hope my research into the subject may help to put the record straight.

Before the New Scheme was introduced, and it had been under discussion since 1859, Welldon had attempted to widen the curriculum by making Maths and French more important, and in particular by appointing Henry Hilary as Head of Maths in 1870, one of the best appointments ever made. Rowe went further by appointing five new masters, including a Science master, and creating a new Chemistry laboratory.

He started to introduce some of the ideas he had developed with Thring. Though a classicist himself, he was aware enough of the new mood in the country to shift the balance from Classics to other subjects. He introduced science classes and gave the Maths department more prominence. He believed in small boarding-houses, and within a few years he approved the opening of two new houses. He inspired the boys' interest in a variety of intellectual areas hitherto ignored, and he prepared to implement the New Scheme when it finally came.

At the same time he created resentment by tightening up some of the school rules. 'When Rowe came to Tonbridge, all that we valued as traditions were objected to and abolished,' one of the Wadmore brothers wrote in later life. He enforced stricter dress rules and tried to reduce the level of noise in the school, particularly at concerts. He banned the use of bicycles, though he eased this restriction later, and he introduced an unpopular rule that if more than 30 boys missed chapel in a week, the next half holiday would be forfeit. On the other hand he eased the rules over bounds and roll-calls. He improved working conditions in School House by creating studies for the junior boys to use in the daytime, so they no longer had to spend their free time sitting in class-rooms, and he made it permissible for senior boys to go to their cubies during the day instead of just at night. He added a corrugated-iron room to the wooden class-rooms in the playground so that at least half the school learnt carpentry, ironwork or instrument-making.

Rowe's main concern was with the intellectual life of the school, but he did not discourage sport, which was experiencing a boom at most public schools. The 1st XI played its first match against the MCC in 1876 and a letter to *The Tonbridgian* complained that there was too much cricket at Tonbridge. Another letter demanded the creation of an OT Cricket Club.

A school museum was established in 1877 and a successful appeal made for exhibits. Bugs, moths, fossils, stones, butterflies and even axes and tomahawks flooded in, so that the specially designed cases in the upper corridor overflowed and the museum was soon looking for larger premises. A special room was promised (in 1991 we are still waiting). An observatory was purchased and erected on the playground and a telescope donated, so that astronomy became, for a time, part of the syllabus. The photographic society was founded and flourished, and over 200 lectures were arranged on every conceivable subject from telepathy to sewage. The lecture on sewage was given by Rowe himself. Playing-fields were extended and levelled, school matches increased in number and house matches introduced. Three concerts a year were held instead of one, and instrumental items were added to choral ones. In 1877 the VIth form sat for exams under the direction of the Oxford and Cambridge Board for the first time. All this was done in spite of the current uncertainty.

In preparation for the introduction of a wider syllabus, the Governors started to look for the money to enlarge the buildings. In 1877 they received a generous offer of help from Edward Cazalet of Fairlawn. He offered to give £10,000 to help build a new Science building or to pay another Science master if the Governors would supply the rest of the money. The Governors could not refuse such a generous offer, but felt that

Old Big School with names on the end wall, c. 1890. The names were panelled over when the room was refurbished in the 1960s.

Roller, horse and groundsmen on School Field Upper Level. The school horse is frequently mentioned in The Tonbridgian, *and various alternative methods of pulling the roller were suggested. Tonbridge has had a series of long-serving groundsmen, one of whom is shown here on the Upper Hundred.*

they could not make a case for such expenditure with the Charity Commissioners. While they were deliberating, Cazalet went to Constantinople to see the Sultan and died there, so the offer lapsed.

Meanwhile the school horse had passed away after many years' service pulling the roller. The new one was almost as decrepit as the old one. 'Why should we become a rest-home for every broken-down cab-horse in the area?' *The Tonbridgian* asked. One reader had the answer. The horse should be disposed of and junior boys harnessed to the roller instead. More seats for the ladies round the Head, a Natural History Society and compulsory football were demanded – not all in the same letter. Other letters said that the foundation of a Boat Club would be the ruination of cricket and complained about the perils of paperchasing (*see opposite*).

In 1877 Hill Side was opened under the housemastership of Mr Langhorne. In 1878 Rowe appointed an ex-pupil from Uppingham to the staff, the Revd. Arthur Lucas, who was to become Chaplain and housemaster of the next new house, Parkside, opened the same year. Lucas was to stay 31 years and prove one of the best masters Tonbridge ever had.

In 1879 Teddy Welldon died. It could not have been easy for Rowe to work with E. I. Welldon as his deputy. Teddy Welldon was a strict disciplinarian, but he did not approve of Rowe's love of fussy detail and liking for sets of rules, and, like his brother, he had a strong following among Old Boys. There is a glowing tribute to his dedication to the school in *The Tonbridgian*. With him the post of Second Master was abolished and was not to be revived for nearly a hundred years.

The New Scheme of 1880 came into effect on 1 January 1881. After this, it was easier to plan ahead. The New Scheme, which is given in detail in 23 pages of Rivington, and was described by *The Tonbridgian* as 'a great anticlimax which made very little difference to anybody', contained the following major ideas:

1. The number of leaving exhibitions was increased to four a year, tenable at any university or college approved by the Governors, and, with one exception, no longer favoured foundationers over non-foundationers – a distinction which had caused more ill-feeling than anything else in the school's history.

2. The curriculum was to be considerably widened and, when possible, extra buildings provided to suit the new timetable.

3. The Governors would in future fix the fees instead of the Headmaster.

4. The Governors would decide how many masters to employ.

5. The age of entry should be raised to 10.

6. The Skinners' Company were to remain sole Governors.

Rowe meanwhile submitted to the Governors ten memoranda, covering every aspect of school life from staff pensions to sanitation, about which he obviously felt strongly as a result of outbreaks of diphtheria at Uppingham. Most of Rowe's ideas were adopted by the Governors. In future there were to be three sides – Classical, Modern and Science. The syllabus was to cover English, Greek, Latin, Maths, Natural Science, French, German, Political Economy, Drawing and Vocal Music.

The argument about the provision of a second-grade school in or near Tonbridge still raged on and was only settled by the Governors agreeing to found two new schools – a second-grade school at Tunbridge Wells, the Skinners' School, which opened in 1887, and a commercial school at Tonbridge, the Judd School, which opened in 1888. The latter was funded by taking £500 a year from the Tonbridge School foundation, obtained by cutting two masters from the Classics department. This again caused resentment, especially as one of those sacked was W. O. Hughes-Hughes, a popular OT.

Both schools were funded by the Skinners' Company, in return for which they were left as sole Governors of Tonbridge; they were one of the few, if not the only, body of governors whose powers were not reduced by the various government commissions.

· Once again the strange anomalies of the school's finances make themselves apparent. While cutting the Classics department to save £500 a year, the Governors were busy trying to raise large sums of money for the new buildings demanded by the scheme. In 1884 Rowe made one of his best appointments – Alfred Earl came to Tonbridge as Head of Science. Earl was a go-getter and an empire-builder, and over the next 34 years created one of the most go-ahead Science departments in the country. Together, he and Rowe changed the school from a classics-centred school to a science one, though the Classics and Modern departments continued to have their share of the really bright boys. Earl was promised a new Science building and took great care to plan it well. He visited several other schools

To the Editors of
The Tonbridgian – 1879

Sir,

Though I am only a little boy I hope you won't mind my writing to you about my first Paper Chase. I ran it last Saturday and feel very disappointed. I had been looking forward to it for a long time. All the fellows had told me how jolly it would be. We had been discussing for the last month who was likely to come in first and some had even gone so far as not to take any pudding for a week. Soon after starting, when I found myself head over ears in a dirty stream, I was not quite so sure whether it was so very jolly after all, but still I hoped that the pleasure would soon come. It did not however. The hares seemed to think that a Paper Chase was not a chase after them, but a sort of game of hide and seek with the paper. They had laid so many false scents, as the fellows called them, that no one could tell where they had gone, but we all kept walking about the fields feeling very cold and wretched. No one even had the pleasure of coming in first, and those who had gone without their pudding were really to be pitied.

Yours obediently

A Small Puppy

and his building, which opened in 1887, is still in use today with surprisingly few alterations.

The new Science building was opened by the Lord Mayor of London, Sir Reginald Hanson (OT) in 1887. The Astronomer Royal of Ireland, Sir Robert Ball, gave a speech in which he said that the learning of Greek and Latin was an absurd waste of time. Dr Welldon, who was in the audience, went back to his parish in Kent, muttering that he hoped Classics were not about to take a back seat. The magnificent new building contained physics, chemistry and biology labs, a drawing-school and a library. It is so solidly built that the only way the school could replace it with a modern building would be to move to a new site.

Thanks to Rowe, staff salaries were improved, regular staff meetings introduced, and a school mission founded in St Pancras – another of Thring's favourite ideas – and blessed with a new church, the Church of the Holy Cross, which opened in 1887.

In 1880 *The Tonbridgian* complained about the sports being ruined by the presence of louts – outsiders who rolled down the bank on to the Head and disrupted the events. The Games Committee was reconstituted to run school sport. It comprised a mixture of masters and boys, but it was dominated by Goggs and Lucas. The first list of the Games Committee listed the captains of cricket and football above the Head Boy, who was still in those days the top scholar in the school.

A house cricket competition was started in 1880, with one master allowed to play for each house, and a tennis competition was held. The 1st XI lost to Lancing for the first time, because they had nothing to eat until the lunch interval! In 1881 rugger house matches began, with Judde House beating the day boys – the first sign of the day boys being able to compete with the boarders. The same year Judde House beat Day boys A–K by one run – the first time a division of the day boys has been mentioned. A dramatic society was founded under Babington, though it was mainly concerned with reading plays rather than acting them. In the rugger match against Dulwich, Tonbridge were awarded a try which would have won the match, but Dulwich protested that the line-out was not straight, and the try was cancelled. Each side had an umpire, but there was no referee, and *The Tonbridgian* complained that matches against Dulwich never passed without incident. In 1881 there were four OTs in the Cambridge XV – all forwards. Possibly the toughness of the old Tonbridge game had survived. J. Le Fleming who played three-quarter for England in 1887 described rugger at Tonbridge in the late 1870s thus:

> The school of 250 was divided into a 50, an Upper 100 and a Lower 100. There were only three grounds. On the Upper 100 there were thirty forwards at least on each side. As a rash youth I once dashed into the middle of the first scrimmage, and it was twenty minutes before I again saw the light of day. I vowed never to do it again and do not think I did.

The Tonbridgian contained a series of sketches about various types of boy

46

in the school – the novi; the fag; the blood – the swell with colours; the bully who came into chapel at the last minute hoping to create an impression; the sloper who spent the whole day 'sloping' – creeping up and down the High Street going from one food shop to another. Complaints were made about the standard of cricket on lower games, lack of facilities for visiting teams, and the proliferation of rings on fingers and buttonholes in Sunday chapel to impress the ladies. Someone wrote and asked why teams at football could not wear distinctive colours, and a young man at Rugby School replied, explaining that all that was necessary was for one team to wear white and the other stripes.

One boy wrote and asked if there could not be a photo of the masters for the boys to take home for the holidays or when they left, and a new Common Room photo of 1883 was offered for sale to the boys! There was a fire in the IVth-form class-room, extinguished by an alert porter.

In 1883 the 'best 1st XI ever' scored 444 against Brighton. C. J. B. Marriott (OT), now captain of Cambridge, and soon to be captain of England, contributed a long article on how to play rugby. In 1884 Rashleigh scored 203 *v.* Dulwich and the 1st XI went on a cricket tour to Holland. The dramatic society performed Sheridan's *The Critic* but the first real play was Bulwer Lytton's *The Lady of Lyons.* Soon after, the dramatic society was dissolved because masters thought acting took up too much time.

In 1884 Day boys A–K won the house cricket, thanks almost entirely to Mr Goggs, who made 53 runs and took 5 wickets. In 1885 School House A–K won the football house matches, Mr Earl scoring 5 tries! The OT Society was formed in 1886 and the Rovers Cricket Club turned into the

Above left. This nineteenth-century photo of tennis being played on the Head must have been taken before the bat fives court was pulled down in 1893 and the wooden classrooms removed in 1894.

Above. This view of the back of the school, c. 1880 shows boys playing bat fives and fags on duty to fetch the ball. Fagging in those days included fetching balls at cricket or fives. The surface of the Head seems surprisingly uneven, compared with that shown in the photo with the tennis players.

Old Tonbridgian Cricket Club. In 1887 the name Kortright first appears in the cricket scores. He was already quite old when he came to the school from Brentwood, and both schools claim him as their own. Many people think he was the fastest bowler ever and was unfortunate not to play for England. In his first season in the XI he took 52 wickets for an average of 11.35, though this was not a record. In 1888 he broke the record by taking 53 wickets for an average of 7.3. *The Tonbridgian* complained that the school colours were being worn by all the townsfolk. By 1889 Tonbridge came fourth in the list of rugger internationals, even though the school was still quite small, and the XV played Bedford for the first time and were thrashed 25–0. Of course 'Bedford is a much bigger school!'

On Skinners' Day Dr Welldon was invited back to speak. 'Tonbridge', he said, 'is the healthiest school, and has the best buildings and best playgrounds in England.' He was comparing it to some London schools which kept having to send the boys home because of illness.

This remark is also a considerable compliment to the achievements of his successor. Unfortunately, however, numbers were dropping, partly because of the raising of the age of entry, and, according to the Governors in a very unkind letter to Rowe, because of the decrepitude of a few of the staff and the Headmaster's own unpopularity. In 1890 Rowe resigned and retired to a parish in Bournemouth, refusing to dismiss masters so near to his own departure. His Old Boys collected for a portrait which now hangs with the others in Big School.

It is hard to agree with Rivington's and Somervell's assessment of him; they give him too little credit for the changes he brought about. He may not have had the appeal of his predecessor, but he obviously thought and cared about his boys and his masters, and, in so far as he tried to implement Thring's ideas at Tonbridge, he had some success. Many years later Old Boys still spoke of him fondly at the OT dinner in London.

In 1931, A. G. B. West, captain of the successful 1883 XI spoke affectionately about the masters in Rowe's day, especially Rowe himself, Babington, Goggs and Hilary.

'As I think of them all now, it is fair for me to say, "By God, how they poured out their life blood for us, those masters giving their energy and their time, and what little blighters most of us were!" They did not lose their patience, and their hearts, and their courage.'

Sir Valentine Ball, speaking two years later, said:

'Tibi, as we called him, treated me as he treated all the boys with the greatest kindness, and I think he was beloved by us all.'

Canon Hugh Le Fleming said that Rowe rarely used the cane, but, when he did, he hurt. Mrs Rowe, who was a very kind and compassionate lady, used to wait in the hall outside the study holding a tray with sherry and biscuits to revive the flagging victim. Another OT said that when he got caned, Mrs Rowe gave him a glass before the beating and a glass afterwards – then perhaps he was a 'blood'.

7

JOSEPH WOOD

'From now on the idle boy is as extinct as the Great Auk!'
Dr Wood, 1897

With Rowe's departure the period of transition from the pre-Scheme days came to an end; the syllabus had been widened and a considerable amount of building done. What was needed now was the right man to increase the numbers to take advantage of the vastly improved facilities. Once again, the Governors either showed the most remarkable skill or had the most extraordinary luck because the man they chose was ideal.

The Revd. Joseph Wood was educated at Manchester Grammar School. He won an exhibition to Balliol where he obtained a first in Greats, and in 1867 he became a master at Cheltenham College. In 1870, at the age of 28, he was appointed Headmaster of Leamington College, where he remained for 20 years and was outstandingly successful. He was also very popular, and, when he was appointed Headmaster of Tonbridge in 1890, he brought with him nearly 100 pupils and masters. Such movement of boys to follow a successful headmaster elsewhere was not unusual in those days, but on such a scale it could only have had a devastating effect on the school they left behind.

J. Wood, by G. Koberwein Terrell.

By the time he came to Tonbridge, Wood had already had 20 years' experience as a headmaster. In his eight years at Tonbridge numbers rose from 174 to 444, so rapidly that *The Tonbridgian* keeps complaining that the school can't cope with the rising numbers.

The main reason for this rapid increase was Wood himself, but the impressive new Science building must have appealed to prospective parents, and a further boost to numbers was given by Wood's immediate decision to change the daily timetable radically. He abolished early school, which up till then had started at 7 a.m. in the summer and 7.30 in the winter. This had meant that it was virtually impossible for any day boys to attend the school who did not live within walking distance.

After 1890, early school was replaced by early preparation, either in a boy's boarding-house or at home. Morning school in future started after

'Cricket on the Head' by F. P. Barraud, 1891. This attempt by Barraud to imitate Dodd's painting, though not so impressive, is remarkable for the fact that the masters, old boys and boys in it are real people and their names are recorded. They include Dr Wood, the Headmaster, E. H. Goggs, H. Hilary, A. Lucas, W. Rashleigh and J. Le Fleming.

chapel at 8.55. Day-boy education at Tonbridge now became possible for those living in Tunbridge Wells and Sevenoaks. By 1898 the number of day boys had increased from 59 to 137, and in 1893 they were divided into two houses. For a short time the division was alphabetical, as it already was for house matches, but soon the division was made geographical – Day boys 'A' for those who lived near the school and were able to take their meals at home, and Day boys 'B' for those who had to have their lunch at school. Each of the day-boy houses was put in the care of a house tutor.

Since then day boys have supplied about a third of the numbers in the school, and their status has steadily improved. The day boys have added considerably to the school, particularly in the intellectual and academic fields. It will probably always be impossible to eliminate the illogical feeling of superiority boarders assume, but in recent years anyway there has been very little of the friction which existed in Welldon's time and beyond. I recently asked a well-known Old Boy if he, as a day boy, had experienced such prejudice while he was in Day boys 'A'. 'Good Lord, no!' he replied, 'We got on very well with the boarders. We were too busy hating Day boys 'B'!'

Another significant change which Wood introduced was one which Rowe had wanted to introduce but failed. Wood persuaded the Governors that the time had come to end the school's weekly attendance at the parish church on Sunday mornings. The Governors agreed that the Founder's wishes in this matter could be met by attending once a year – on Skinners' Day. *The Tonbridgian* greeted this change with glee. No longer would it be necessary to traipse through the mud and sit through endless sermons with soaking wet feet.

As a consequence of the rapid increase in numbers, Welldon's school chapel soon became far too small for current needs, and Wood and many other people expressed their wish for a new chapel large enough to seat a school of 450 or more. Preliminary enquiries proved futile. The Charity Commissioners, who were prepared to sanction the school's requests to be allowed to build a gymnasium and swimming-bath, thought that a chapel was not necessary for the boys' education.

Wood's solution was to erect a temporary chapel. The school had already bought Ferox Place, immediately opposite Ferox Hall; it was a row of small cottages, one of which had been Card's, which served as a private tuck-shop. These buildings were now demolished and a temporary corrugated-iron chapel erected on the site. It was quite spacious inside, and later it was enlarged to seat 530. *The Tonbridgian* quipped that it was a building suitable for the Iron Age.

The chapel was not the only building which was bursting at the seams – so were almost all the other buildings, including the boarding-houses. It is probably best here to explain how the boarding-house system worked, because Tonbridge, more than most schools is very much a house-orientated school. A visitor to the school might well find that it is, at first glance, remarkably small, compared say with Wellington or Cranleigh or even Haileybury, where the boarding-houses form part of the main school building. The new schools of the nineteenth century were purpose-built in large open-country sites. The town schools of the Tudor Age had to expand bit by bit, as nearby houses or sites became available.

At Tonbridge, the boarding- and day-houses are scattered in the vicinity of the school – each in its own grounds, but most of them are out of sight of the main building. Those of us who have grown up with this system appreciated the benefit of going home to a different environment in the evening, especially as most houses have their own tennis-courts or play areas and gardens.

Back in the 1890s boarding-houses were either owned or rented by the housemaster and he took the profits, which were not great. Park House, which was opened in 1867, went on the market in 1890, and no one on the staff was either rich enough or rash enough to take it on, so H. R. Stokoe, who was not on the staff, bought it and is reputed to have sent the Headmaster a letter, saying 'I have purchased Park House and will be joining your staff next term.' This seems extraordinary, but Stokoe duly arrived, joined the staff and ran Park House for 41 years. In 1891 he enlarged Little's building considerably and increased the number of boarders to 40.

Ferox Hall was opened as a boarding-house by Mr Earl in 1892 and Manor House by Mr Pott in 1894. Both of these houses were famous old Tonbridge buildings, whose histories are recorded in Gilbert Hoole's book. They have both been enlarged over the years. In 1893 Judde House, which had outgrown its quarters in Old Judde where it had been based since 1825, moved to new premises on the London Road under Mr Whitby. Old Judde

The temporary chapel, 1892–1902. Known as the 'Tin Tabernacle', it was afterwards given to the Judd School for use as a workshop. One day it caught fire and Bill Werren, the Clerk of Works, was summoned and put out the fire, for which he was soundly rebuked by the surveyor, who said the insurance was worth far more than the building.

Ferox Hall in 1879 before it was rebuilt. A house on this site possibly existed as early as the thirteenth century. Since then the building had been altered considerably. During one of the reconstructions the royal coat of arms, containing the letters ER, was found in one of the bedrooms, and it is claimed that Queen Elizabeth slept here. During the ownership of the Children family 1750–1816, George Children used the building to carry out experiments on batteries and gunpowder and frequently entertained Sir Humphry Davy, who injured his eye in one of their experiments.

The building was almost completely rebuilt in 1879 and was purchased by Mr Earl as a boarding-house in 1892.

then underwent the first of its many changes of use and was converted into the sanatorium.

The 1880s and 1890s were not only a time of expansion in buildings. They were also the period when changes in staff became more frequent and more significant. It is the time when masters started to take on flesh and bone in the pages of the various histories. We have already heard of Goggs and Hilary, Earl and Lucas, Whitby and Stokoe. The days of Towers' visiting French and dancing-masters were over. There was now a solid core of masters who came to Tonbridge for their whole careers, and, as in most schools, they were far more important than the buildings, though the Governors were slow to grasp this.

'Toddy' Goggs retired in 1896 after 34 years as a Maths master and continued for another 35 years as a monument to Victorian grandeur until, at the age of 95, he was knocked down in the cattle-market by an unruly bullock. In his retirement he became the leading figure on Sports Day on the Head; as referee he entertained the judges, all distinguished OT athletes, to a champagne lunch and then, helped up into an armchair standing on a large table by the finishing-tape, he kept a watchful eye on the proceedings. He was hardly ever called on to make a decision other than on the famous occasion when a sensationally fast time was recorded for the Mile, and it was found to have ended a lap short.

Wood, with his constantly increasing numbers, seemed to have the Governors in his pocket, if not the Charity Commissioners. Moreover the school's reputation was growing in other areas, particularly sport, helped by exceptionally successful XIs in 1883 and 1893 and a growing number of OT rugger internationals.

52

The pressure on space led in 1894 to the last and most ambitious phase of the building programme begun in 1863. The gap between the 1863 building and the new Science building was closed by the construction of what was then called the New Building, consisting of a large central tower and a new block containing several large new class-rooms, a basement to which the workshops were moved and new cubies and studies for School House on the top floor. The old wooden classrooms in the playground were removed.

At the back of the school a spacious hall, called Big School, was built, with seating for 450 and a large stage at one end. There were galleries at both ends, with an organ in the further gallery. This is still, 100 years later, the school's main assembly hall, though for many years it has been too small to seat the whole school together.

The tower, with its large clock, provided a spacious room as a Masters' Common Room. This room is right at the heart of the school, with tall, wide windows looking out on the High Street to the east and across the Head to the west. It was opened in 1894, and the Common Room minutes date from that time. The first page contains a few simple rules – 'no smoking and no bridge: subscription 5s'.

The Archbishop of Canterbury opened the building and Wood was able to wax eloquent about the class-rooms. 'The migratory period is now over. Until now one master has been teaching in the Cricket Pavilion, one in the Gymnasium and one in a fives court.' Referring to the new work-shops, he made his famous comment on the facilities now provided by the school: 'In the future the idle boy will be as extinct as the Great Auk.'

Wood's building programme was not yet complete and the mind can hardly take in how much was being done in such a short space of time. In 1897 the swimming-bath was opened in the Hadlow Road – a long way from the school – even farther than the Medway, but the praes' privilege of cycling there became a strong incentive to become a prae, and it was a well-planned pool with plenty of room for sunbathing. It was never heated however, and, as the summer term got earlier, it became usable for a shorter time each year and was replaced by an indoor heated pool in 1975.

The rackets court, for which *The Tonbridgian* had been pleading for years, was opened in 1897. The money was raised by subscription in honour of Jack Dale, a famous Tonbridge sportsman. At the same time Martin's Fields were leased, increasing the number of pitches available. Jack Dale, then aged 22, once scored 55 in a partnership of 164 with W. G. Grace for the Gentlemen *v.* Players at the Oval.

In 1898 Wood was appointed Headmaster of Harrow and one is left to wonder how much he would have achieved, had he stayed. Plans for the chapel were already well advanced – it was just a question of the Charity Commissioners granting permission and the Governors finding or borrowing the money. The Charity Commissioners were at last persuaded to relent, possibly because their churlish attitude over the chapel had led to awkward questions about Tonbridge school chapel in the House of

Below. *Old Judde House from the back, 1893. Judde House was the second house to be opened – in 1826. It remained in Old Judde until it moved to its present premises in 1893.*

Bottom. *This picture shows Old Judde as it was before its rear wing was pulled down to make way for the new buildings which were built across its garden in 1894.*

When the main school building was completed in 1894, there was much talk of pulling down Old Judde and Welldon's chapel. This drawing by Mr Campbell-Jones, the school architect, shows what the front of the school would look like without them. Fortunately, the idea was dropped.

Commons. The Governors agreed to borrow money on the prospect of increasing funds from the endowment after 1906. The sums of money they had spent since 1863 were staggering: it meant entering the twentieth century with considerable debts – but at last the school had premises worthy of it.

Now in an attempt to add a more human touch to this scene of frantic activity, let us go back to 1890. Tonbridge town had been growing steadily since the coming of the railways and new estates were growing up in the Hadlow Road and Dry Hill Park areas. Most of the private houses were for the new commuting or professional classes, who would hope to send their sons to the school. In 1898 A. L. Bickmore, a master at Tonbridge, opened Yardley Court Prep School, with Wood's encouragement.

The upsurge in activity is reflected in several areas. The 1st XI of 1893 was declared by C. B. Fry in *Wisden* to be one of the three best school XIs of that year. The choir had a dynamic new Director of Music, Dr Brewer, who went on to become organist of Gloucester Cathedral, Director of the Three Choirs Festival and a knight. Under him the choir was invited to

Smoking, which used to be compulsory at some schools to ward off infection, has always been illegal at Tonbridge. This photo, entitled 'Cats away' shows that boys have not changed. A day boy's diary of this period records that while his friend was beaten for smoking by Dr Wood, he was merely given thirty days' extra cricket.

sing at Canterbury Cathedral, and Brewer was congratulated for playing the cathedral organ with so much gusto that he broke the record for the amount of water used by the hydraulic apparatus.

From 1891 *The Tonbridgian* suddenly becomes much more lively, reflecting the new spirit of development, though it devotes most of its space to sport, and the school in this decade and the following one showed a tendency to philistinism, echoing the national mood with its passion for Empire and its worry about the Boers. Wood, a keen sportsman himself, reduced the number of 1st XV matches to twelve. He was also a strict disciplinarian, and he used the cane frequently, even beating his own son for going into the quad without his cap on. He instituted a new system of making absentees report to him personally the day they returned. This probably cut absenteeism at a stroke.

Electric light was installed in most of the rooms except, oddly, in the library, where the gas-burners continued to raise complaints. Drill was discontinued as a punishment; instead boys had to pull the roller. A new tuck-shop was built, owned by the school, 'selling jam, eggs and sardines'. A new handicap race to Shipbourne and back was introduced – to be run four times a year, with a handicap of 10 seconds per month according to the age of the competitor. Cricket became compulsory, and *The Tonbridgian* complained that compulsory cricket and voluntary rugger did not make sense, so rugger became compulsory too, thereby boosting the position of *The Tonbridgian*. Until the building of the new Big School, the school took over the Public Hall in the High Street for the Skinners' Day prize-giving.

The school had a new cricket professional – Alec Hearne of Kent – and there were four Old Boys in the Kent XI. The 1st XI made scores of 439, 445 and 451 against St Paul's, Brighton and the OTs respectively. The 1st XI had a new blazer and swimmers wore red and non-swimmers white drawers. Rowing and golf clubs were established and the playing-fields renamed with the names by which we know them today. The cricket pavilion was enlarged and water polo introduced. House suppers are mentioned for the first time, even for the day boys.

But not everything was perfect according to *The Tonbridgian*. In 1890 the times achieved in the athletic sports were awful, and it was discovered that all the distances had been wrongly measured – the 100 yards, for example, was found to measure 106 yards. Someone suggested that it was wrong for the school to have to pay the expenses of visiting teams. There was a row about masters playing in house matches. The boys voted for the system to continue, but the masters decided that if they were selected, they would refuse to play! The boys complained that too little time was available for practice because masters kept keeping boys in. Under the new timetable the school was free to go swimming at 12 noon, under the watchful eye of the Head Porter, but the swimming-bath was not yet built and *The Tonbridgian* continued to complain about dead cats and dogs in the Medway.

Corps Inspection, 1897. One of the earliest photos of the Corps, showing the original uniforms and the old fives courts.

In its early years the Corps was attached to the 1st Middlesex Royal Engineer Volunteers and the emphasis was on engineering. This photo shows the cadets building the path connecting the quad to the cricket pavilion in 1894.

The worst things were the new school caps in house colours which made Tonbridgians look like 'errand boys'. And worse was to follow. In 1892 it was discovered, to universal horror, that the cricket chain which had been used for the last 25 years for measuring pitches was six inches too long. At most schools this might not matter. At Tonbridge it was a major disaster. Moreover, no one knew how long this had been going on. Had it suddenly stretched, or was it too long to start with? How many good-length balls had fallen short? As for matches: Haileybury, it was claimed, were much better hosts than Tonbridge. (I think they still are.)

The 1st XV, having been thrashed by Bedford, *The Tonbridgian* pleaded for the school to have a proper rugger coach like Bedford, so R. L. Aston, a famous OT rugger international was appointed to the staff and the 1st XV immediately benefited from his coaching. (Somewhere I read that the school full-back converted 55 tries in one season, but only one penalty goal. I cannot find my note on this and do not know which year it was – 1895 or 1905? Or who it was?)

In 1897 the magnificent new Fifty ground at the Elms was leased. Three new cricket fields were brought into use, and Cecil Wilson, an OT and Kent cricketer was appointed Bishop of Melanesia and introduced cricket to the Melanesians. There have been regular collections in chapel for the Melanesian Mission ever since, presumably to provide more kit. Several OT cricketers played for Kent, including Rashleigh who topped the Kent averages in 1893. F. A. Jackson played rugger for Kent, golf for Leicestershire and tennis for Norfolk.

In Welldon's time there had been a Volunteer Corps, but it did not last long. In 1892 permission was obtained from the War Office for formation of a School Cadet Corps. Initially limited to 100 boys, the limit was regularly increased until it reached 360, 15 years later, reflecting the political uncertainties of the time.

The school received its first royal visit in the persons of Prince and Princess Henry of Battenberg. Under Herbert Brewer an orchestra was formed, a Glee Club was founded and school song concerts became a regular feature. The new XV song ('Sing hey! for the Gutter and for glory!') was sung after the first match against Sherborne ended in victory. A range was built for the Corps; the school had its first inspection and its first camp at Aldershot, and shooting-cups and competitions and participation at Bisley reflected the growing concern with military matters. The school engineer squad built the road from the quad to the armoury and the path from the quad to the pavilion which are still used today. *The Tonbridgian* raised its price from 6*d.* to 9*d.* – the first rise since 1858 – and dropped to six issues a year. In 1893 it published a list of the school rules.

The boys wrote to the Duke of York, later George V, congratulating him on the birth of his son, later Edward VIII, and asking him for an extra week's holiday, which he ordered the Headmaster to grant.

In 1895 the first regular school printed list, such as we know it today appeared. The boys complained of the rigours of having to drill at 7 a.m.

and the Archbishop of Canterbury took confirmation in the temporary chapel; the first school play – *Old Soldiers* by Byron – was performed. On 25 December 1896 Dr Welldon died at the age of 85.

In 1897 the Tonbridge School contingent led the Diamond Jubilee march past of 3,000 cadets in front of Queen Victoria in Windsor Great Park – a very great honour.

In 1897, also, E. M. Forster left after four years, and in the light of the recent increase in his popularity through films of *A Passage to India*, *A Room with a View* and *Maurice* something must be said about his time at Tonbridge, especially as both Rivington and Somervell chose to ignore him. He is reputed to have hated his time at school, though this has never been proved, and is a reputation based on his attack on public schools in *The Longest Journey* and a lecture of which we do not have a copy. His fictitious school Sawston is a set of values as well as a place on a map. It represents upper-middle-class suburbia, the stronghold of orthodoxy, convention and chauvinism. However, Forster did win the Latin and English Essay prizes, which he had to read aloud on Skinners' Day, and he voluntarily became a life member of the Old Tonbridgian Society at a time when this was not the normal thing to do. Space prevents my devoting longer to this interesting subject, but there is no doubt that Tonbridge under Wood was not a school for loners, especially day-bugs who did not like games.

His contemporary, Edmund Ironside, who had a very different view of his schooldays, had meanwhile passed into Woolwich. W. Alexander was made Archbishop of Armagh and Primate of All Ireland – the first, but not the last, OT Archbishop. His wife, Mrs Alexander, the hymn-writer, is now more famous than her husband.

In 1898 the Charity Commissioners sanctioned the spending of £15,000 on a new chapel, and a letter to *The Tonbridgian* complained because it was going to be built of red brick and would not match the school buildings. The OTs had their first cricket week, and prep schools were mentioned for the first time in the scholarship lists.

In 1898 Joseph Wood moved on to Harrow. The school had never had such a period of rapid growth and change. Somervell, who was a boy at Harrow under Wood and liked him enormously, says he lost a little of his attention to detail in his latter years at Harrow, which is hardly surprising after so many years of headmastering at such a tempo. When he left Harrow in 1910, he had been a headmaster for 40 years. Later memories of OTs pay him glowing tributes, well echoed in his obituary in *The Times* of 1923.

> Tonbridgians cannot forget all that he did for their School and the success that attended his work there. He was a tall man with fine features, a wonderful 'presence' and a great charm of manner, and those who worked under him, whether as masters or boys, can never forget his wonderful personality and the feeling with which they regarded him as their Headmaster.

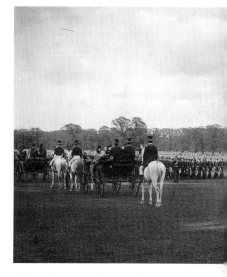

Jubilee Parade, Windsor Great Park, 1897. Tonbridge contingent leading. Tonbridge had the honour of leading the parade of 3,000 cadets. Queen Victoria can just be seen in her carriage.

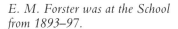

E. M. Forster was at the School from 1893–97.

8

CHARLES TANCOCK

The Praepostorial System may be justly regarded as the most distinctive feature of the great public schools of England.

The Tonbridgian: *Editorial, 1901*

C. C. Tancock, by Henry Tuke, ARA.

The last two decades of the nineteenth century had seen far more changes in every area of school life than the previous 300 years. In 1899 the school badly needed a period of calm and consolidation. This is in no way a criticism of Dr Wood, but, as his successor, the Governors chose a very different type of man.

The Revd. Charles Tancock DD was a Cornishman. Born in 1851, he went to Sherborne, a school with which Tonbridge had already established sporting links and whose history was very similar. At Sherborne he was Head Boy and captain of cricket and rugger. He won a scholarship to Exeter College, Oxford, where he obtained a 1st in Classics. He was ordained and, for 11 years, was an assistant master at Charterhouse. In 1886 he was appointed Headmaster of Rossall and during his 10 years there, Rossall achieved its most successful period to date. Unfortunately, Tancock believed in working harder than everybody else, and in 1896 he had to retire from Rossall through ill-health. He spent a short time running a small parish in Westmorland, and in 1899, having apparently recovered his health, he was appointed Headmaster of Tonbridge.

He lacked Wood's energy and dynamism, but he was universally popular and regarded as a considerate Headmaster and a kindly friend. He loved teaching, and it was seen as a privilege to be in one of his Greek or Ancient History classes. He was clearly the ideal man to give the school the period of calm it needed.

However, the outside world was changing rapidly, and his headmastership was conducted against the background of the South African War and the first signs of the coming European conflict. He was a firm believer in the Cadet Corps and the value of sport, regarding membership of the former as a patriotic duty. In 1899 the Mitchell house cup for efficiency was introduced in memory of a young OT, M. D. Mitchell. The Corps was increasing rapidly in size and importance, and this inevitably affected the school routine. In 1907 Lord Haldane's army reforms converted all the Volunteer Corps into the OTC, with closer links with the Army.

Tancock was devoted to the Classics, but he believed in the importance of the Modern and Science sides and took steps to strengthen the Maths side under Hilary. He was very active on HMC committees, and in 1903 the HMC, for the first time, held its annual conference at Tonbridge, a conference remembered for two proposals:

1. That the public schools should introduce a Common Entrance examination.

2. That they should abolish the study of Euclid's *Elements* in favour of the study of modern Geometry.

Tancock was highly regarded for his knowledge of education and he was a gifted preacher. He was made an honorary canon of Rochester Cathedral and he became chief adviser to the Kent Education Committee.

Rivington and Hart do not devote much space in their histories to Tancock's headmastership, the implication being that it was merely an interlude between two much busier periods. This judgement is questionable because a great deal did happen at the school, although it was overshadowed by the turbulent international background. During his time the school had considerable success both in the class-room and on the games field, and the number of scholarships obtained each year at Oxford and Cambridge far exceeded previous achievements and was unsurpassed for the next 60 years. There were several successful school teams at both cricket and rugger, and the number of OT county and international players is remarkable. Other sports began to feature in the school's programme, and large areas of additional playing-fields were purchased, showing commendable foresight either by Tancock or by the Governors.

The two chief features of his reign were inevitably the South African War and the building of the new chapel. With permission from the Charity Commissioners to expend £15,000 on the new chapel, the Governors decided it should be built in two phases. The £15,000 should be spent on the main part of the building, with the rest to be added later when more funds were available. The cost of providing the furnishings, fittings and windows etc. estimated at £2,000 was to be met by private appeal.

The foundation stone of the chapel was laid in 1900 by the Master of the Skinners' Company, Mr Jeremiah Colman, of mustard fame, and, prior to the dedication ceremony, at a service in the parish church, the sermon was preached by the Archbishop of Canterbury, Dr Temple. The planned procession to the site was ruined by heavy rain, but eventually the Master laid the stone, beneath which a glass bottle was deposited, containing some 1900 coins, and copies of *The Times* and *The Tonbridgian*.

The first stage of the building, designed by Mr W. Campbell Jones, cost £17,827, leaving the last two bays – where the organ-loft, ante-chapel, vestry and cloisters were to go – to be completed when funds would allow. A screen was erected to hide the hole in the west end. *The Tonbridgian*

complained that it looked very ugly and that the missing part would cost a further £10,000 to complete. On 26 May 1902, St Augustine of Canterbury's chapel, still only two-thirds built, was consecrated by the Archbishop, at a combined service of consecration and communion.

In the light of the awful tragedy which was later to strike this building, the repository of so many men's dreams and memories, it is both pointless and too painful to describe the chapel in detail. Rivington gives detailed plans of the building, the windows and the fittings in his fourth edition, which can be found in the school library. Suffice it to say here that, when it was built, it was not without controversy. It dominated its site almost to the exclusion of the main school building behind it. It was built predominantly of red brick and faced with stone; the bricks were of different shades and in bands, to give it a glowing effect, but there were some, including W. G. Hart, who thought it was a pity that it could not be built entirely of stone to match the main buildings. Yet once the building had settled into its background and mellowed a little, the contrast of brick and stone became a natural part of the scenery, especially when viewed from the far side of the Head on a summer evening. Inside it was very impressive, especially after it was completed in 1909. Several of the best features were added later, but the beauty of the windows, the richness of the wood, the overwhelming feeling of dignity are never to be forgotten. Even Hart, in his history, having criticized it, goes on to quote Arthur Mee's *Kent*. Mee was writing several years after the war, but his final comment on the chapel is worth giving at this point:

> The best modern building for miles around is this, the place from which the Tonbridge boys went out to France.

In 1902 the Great War and its awful consequences were still 12 years away, and in those days it was the war in South Africa which filled the newspapers. *The Tonbridgian* contained a list of those serving in South Africa and published several long letters from J. Le Fleming, who was serving there, written to his father:

We are all determined to make the crafty Boer rue the day when the war began. A reverse like we had at Colenso does not affect Tommy's spirits in the least: he only wants to get at the Boer with the bayonet. If you hear a word spoken against Tommy, I hope you will sit on the speaker well: his conduct is always one thing, and that is gallant. Most of the Boer bullets are very humane, and, unless you are hit through the heart or brain, you stand an excellent chance of pulling through. The Boer guns are excellent and their shells rotten, a lot of them not bursting at all. From our camp we always put a few lyddite shells into their trenches every day, about five miles off, 'serving them up with hot meals', as Tommy calls it.

The jubilation over Mafeking in 1900 was as wild in Tonbridge as everywhere else and greater than any experienced later in the two World Wars. *The Tonbridgian* describes it in detail:

Though, of course, discipline prevented the school from taking any part in the nocturnal festivities, there was little sleep for anyone, and the houses re-echoed with vociferous cheers till an early hour in the morning. On Saturday morning there was a general rush down town to secure flags and bunting, and by half-past eight there was scarcely a boy to be seen without some emblem of patriotic enthusiasm. Soon after, or rather during, breakfast time, Parkside could be seen crowded on a brake and proceeding round the park (Dry Hill Park), escorted on every side by a cavalcade of bicycles, and cheering lustily the while. They were soon joined by the rest of the school.

In 1899 Tonbridge played Clifton at cricket for the first time and lost. Cricket leagues and junior house matches were established, and rugger adopted the league system soon after. In December the final house match was postponed because of frost, and those that left that month were allowed to play in the rearranged match the following term. Hockey was introduced in Lent term for all except the top rugger players, and compulsory house runs were introduced on winter half-holidays for those not playing rugger or hockey. In 1901 there were eight OTs in the Kent XV, and C. T. Scott and A. Barr were on opposite sides in the England v. Ireland match. The first school rackets professional, F. P. Fair, was appointed in 1898, and in 1901 K. L. Hutchings and A. K. Boyd reached the semi-final of the Public Schools Rackets at Queen's. Complaints were already being made that we would never win Queen's until the rugger authorities abandoned their prior claim on the best players.

In 1901 Corps became compulsory and annual inspections *de rigueur*, with the fife and drum band leading the march past. Final figures showed that 112 OTs served in South Africa and 12 died, including Mounteney Kortright, C. S. Kortright's younger brother. In 1905 the South African War memorial window in the chapel was unveiled at the same time as the Dr Welldon memorial window.

In 1901 Queen Victoria died, and *The Tonbridgian* surpassed itself in extolling her virtues and regretting the passing of an era. Next year, when the Boers surrendered, the school was given a let-out and the corps fired a *feu de joie*.

In 1903 the school won the Ashburton Shield at Bisley for the first (and

The winning Ashburton Shield VIII, 1903. Tonbridge's successful VIII was greeted at the station by the whole school and most of the town.

last) time: their score of 500 was a record. Charterhouse objected to the final result, claiming that we had used unauthorized rifles, and, though the objection was overruled, the rifles were banned for the future! The Shooting VIII was welcomed home at the station by a large crowd of both schoolboys and townspeople, *The Tonbridgian*, naturally, devoting pages to the event:

> The triumphal return of the VIII with the Shield was a very stirring affair. The spontaneity, heartiness and absolute beauty of welcome were remarkable. . . . The crowd was enormous, and great difficulty was experienced in getting all ready. . . . The VIII were received with a 'General Salute', and conducted to the brake, which was magnificently decorated and harnessed by fourteen members of the School, and driven by the celebrated 'Morley', who must have enjoyed hugely his strange experience in handling a 'team'.

The Shooting VIII of 1907 wearing the new uniforms.

Back at school more speeches were made and more shooting-cups presented in honour of the event. Surprisingly, at the OT Dinner, Tancock, aiming his criticisms at the Government rather than the Governors, deplored the lack of ranges, weapons and ammunition. He even proposed that the Ashburton Shield should be abolished, because the team's practice sessions used up too much of the school's limited supply of ammunition, whereas all boys in the school should have the opportunity to learn to shoot – strange sentiments for a clergyman with a reputation for gentleness!

Against this background the school entered the twentieth century, and there were several new developments, though reports of musical and dramatic activities do seem to be sadly lacking from the pages of *The*

Tonbridgian. Much of the boys' free time was spent in debating. The
Debating Society voted in favour of compulsory games and in 1900 there
was such an uproar at one debate that the school, that is, non-members of
the Society, was in future excluded from attendance. Unfortunately, *The
Tonbridgian* doesn't say what the motion was. Membership of the OT
Society was rising, and Tancock endeared himself to the Old Boys by
providing dinner in Big School each year on the first evening of the OT
cricket match. This was in addition to the yearly OT Dinner in London
which was now attracting attendances of about 100. OT Dinners were also
reported from Melbourne and Buenos Aires.

The Tonbridgian contains an interview with the Corps Sgt.-Maj. C. G.
Latimer RE – the first published interview with anyone working at the
school. It also contains its usual odd mixture of editorials and letters casting
some light on life in the school at that time. Can't we have house colours?
Can't we have athletics matches? Can't we have hockey matches?
Throwing lemons at half-time (to the players, not at them) is a deplorable
habit. There are too many bad umpires. Playing hockey on the quad is
ruining the surface. The use of alphabetical order is discriminatory. . . .

In 1903 Tancock was able to report what he called a marvellous year:
11 scholarships to Oxford and Cambridge in 1902; all school rugger
matches won; the first rowing match against Winchester; P. D. Kendall
captaining the England XV – and the winning of the Ashburton Shield. It
was indeed a rosy patch. For the first time the XV beat all four school
opponents – Dulwich, Haileybury, Sherborne and St Paul's. The OTs
organized a rugger tour to Bath – a fixture they would hardly contemplate

The Cras used to start in the London Road.

Below. *Boys jumping into the River Medway on Skinners' Day. It was traditional, though voluntary, for the boys, in assorted styles of dress and carrying birch boughs, to march down to the river before breakfast and jump in, led by the Head of School.*

Below right. *Boys marching up the High Street after their Skinners' Day swim.*

these days. The Boat Club moved to a new boat-house below the town and regular races against Winchester and King's, Canterbury were organized. The first cross-country race, not yet known by its later name of 'the Cras', took place in 1905, replacing the old steeplechase, and the first race was won by E. S. Dougall, who went on to win a running blue at Cambridge and become Tonbridge's first VC in the Great War.

During this period the school's endowment income was rising substantially with renewal of the London leases, though not as much as Mr Gladstone had predicted in the House of Commons. In 1905 the old temporary chapel was removed and given to the Judd School as a gymnasium and workshop; many years later it caught fire. The Clerk of Works, Bill Werren, was summoned and put the fire out, only to be reprimanded by the surveyor, who said the insurance money was worth far more than the building.

In 1907 the Governors built a new row of seven fives-courts alongside the miniature range and rebuilt the fives-court block on the Lower Hundred, incorporating one squash-court at each end of the doubles-fives-courts. The new Baths fields were already in use by 1900, and in 1904 the fields which had been hired at the Elms (the Fifty) and in the Shipbourne Road, were purchased. Finally in 1907 a new tuck-shop was built, which is now in use as the school shop. With a new chapel and a new tuck-shop, new fives-courts, new playing-fields and new fixtures, Tancock can hardly be said to have been idle.

In 1904 14 scholarships were won, and the school was noted in this period for the success of its boys in the entrance exam to the RMA, Woolwich, at a time when this was highly competitive. It does not seem to have been a period entirely calm and consolidating, though one is still left with this nagging feeling that it was more than a little philistine. A very long and informative letter to *The Tonbridgian*, 50 years later, from G. Seymour Thompson, a keen amateur musician, describes the music facilities in his time, 1896–1900, as awful and the teaching as variable:

64

When I left I was accounted one of the School's principal musicians. My public appearances were confined almost entirely to house suppers and accompanying the hymns on a miniature harmonium.

Tancock seems to have been a popular leader, never happier than when he was watching Tonbridge playing Sherborne on the Fifty. In the end, unfortunately, at the close of 1906, his health broke down again, and he announced his resignation. H. S. Vere Hodge joined the staff during Tancock's time and left some notes 'for the benefit of future historians'. Tancock, he said, was too gentle and sensitive to be a Headmaster. He once retired to his room for three days because he was so upset at having to expel a boy.

In Tancock's absence, Mr Lucas, the senior housemaster, was appointed acting Headmaster. His brief tenure was marked by two significant events. First, the school received a visit from Prince Albert, afterwards George VI. M. S. David, one of the school's best Maths masters, went to London regularly to tutor Prince Edward, and invited Prince Albert down to Tonbridge. A cricket match and a tea-party were laid on for the young prince, and there is a marvellous picture of him sitting with the boys and the Lucases at tea. Secondly, the proceedings on Skinners' Day in 1907 were opened by the firing of a cannon.

Tancock was not able to return to the school before he left in July 1907. Instead he wrote a moving farewell letter to the boys, whom he clearly loved, which was published in *The Tonbridgian*.

1st IV – 1910 – rowing against Mr Rayner's IV. One of the earliest pictures of the 1st IV. The first recorded race, against Winchester, was in 1903.

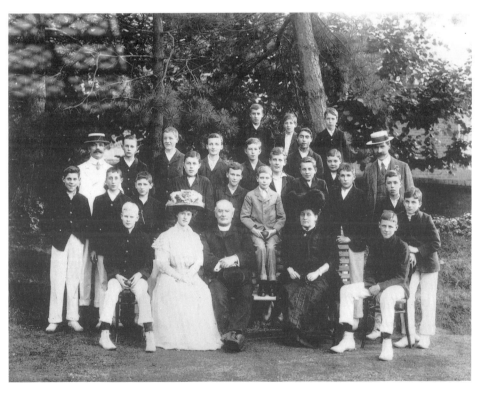

The cricket match with Prince Albert, 1907. In 1907 Mr M. S. David, a Maths master, was a friend of the royal tutor, and used to help with Prince Edward's maths tuition on a part-time basis. He became friendly with Prince Albert, later George VI, who was reputedly a rather shy and lonely boy. Mr David arranged for the Prince to spend a day at the school with his tutor and organized a cricket match with 21 other small boys. Mr David is at the back on the left, and the Prince in the middle. Mr Lucas was acting Headmaster and is shown with Mrs Lucas.

9

CHARLES LOWRY

The trousers were returned in a neat parcel with an accompanying ode as I sat at tea in School House Dining Hall about 6.30.

Letter from W. L. Clarke, 1947

C. Lowry, by Spencer Watson, ARA.

When Dr Tancock became ill at the end of 1906, Mr Lucas was appointed acting Headmaster for two terms while the Governors looked for a successor to Tancock. Once again the Governors showed remarkable skill in their choice, but at the same time they departed from tradition by choosing only the second layman to be Headmaster.

Charles Lowry was born in Gloucestershire in 1857: at the age of ten he won a scholarship to Eton and from Eton he won a classical scholarship to Corpus Christi College, Oxford: at Eton and Oxford he was a leading oarsman. In 1883 he returned to Eton as a master and became Master in College and later a boarding-house master, as well as commander of the Eton Rifle Corps.

In 1900 he was appointed Headmaster of Sedbergh, and during his seven years there the school flourished and he was said to like the simple life at Sedbergh. He married and had two daughters and a son, who later obtained a 1st in Greats and won the Diamond Sculls at Henley.

It may seem strange to start this chapter on Lowry's headmastership by referring to his obituaries, but he was Headmaster for a long time – from 1907 until 1922 – and during possibly the most stressful period in any school's history, that of the Great War. When he died just after his retirement in 1922, his obituary in the *Eton Chronicle* spoke of his great popularity, and a quotation from it may reveal the type of personality which was to steer Tonbridge through such troubled times:

> I believe that he never had an enemy, I am very sure that he never failed a friend: all who knew him loved him, if only because he loved them first: there are some still living to whom the name of Lowry means more than any other Eton name.

The appointment of a lay Headmaster was not the disaster some had predicted. Lowry made his commitment to the chapel clear by preaching at least twice a term, a tradition continued by Headmasters until very recently. He infused a fresh spirit of energy, and was said to combine Eton's wide outlook with Sedbergh's rugged image. He encouraged praepostors to take a high view of their position and responsibilities. He pleased the staff by showing a desire to improve their salaries and introduce a pension scheme. He was a keen supporter of the Corps and his arrival coincided with the establishment of the OTC. He encouraged the Boat Club and frequently coached the 1st IV himself, endearing himself to the boys, as other Tonbridge masters have done, by cycling into the river Medway while coaching. The letter quoted above was written by a School House boy who hesitantly lent him his trousers after one such incident, probably when Lowry was nearly 60.

Somervell, using someone else's headmaster-grading tests, said that a Headmaster should either be able to teach, preach or manage, and, if he could not do any of those, he should be either a scholar or a gentleman. Applying the test to Lowry he gave him reasonable marks for teaching and preaching and scholarship, low marks for organization but top marks for being a gentleman. Fortunately for Lowry, he had some excellent organizers at his elbow in Lucas, Earl and W. M. Gordon. He was criticized for having too fiery a temper and giving too many half-holidays.

One of his innovations was the tutor system, based largely on the Eton practice. All boys were allocated in groups of three or four to a tutor whom they visited once a week in the evening for an hour. Lowry's only proviso was that school work should not form part of these tutor sessions. Unfortuately no one told Mr Wright this: he just sat boys down to do their prep and left the room. The tutor system at Tonbridge has proved of great value to many boys and many masters, though not all. Tutors and tutor-boys frequently stay in touch for years afterwards. A recent housemaster, Gifford Wood, once summed it up thus: 'There are A tutors and B tutors: there are A tutor-boys and B tutor-boys: so the chances of getting the right combination are one in four.' Many would put it nearer one in two: when it works it is an excellent system which still flourishes in an adapted fashion.

Lowry was a keen supporter of the School Mission in St Pancras and chaired the Committee of the Mission which agreed in 1909 to set up a Boys' Club in St Pancras and lease suitable premises in Cromer St.

Perhaps the area where Lowry suited Tonbridge's needs best, though some might claim the opposite, was that he was keen on sport of all types. Reading through issues of *The Tonbridgian* of this period one might think that nothing but sport mattered. Political issues were debated, early hints of German ambitions appear in its pages, and there was a strong overtone of duty to King and Empire, but, as in Tancock's time, there is a sad lack of information about or interest in the arts. Plays were few and far between, and though there was some music and a keen Director of Music in H. C. Stewart, he was short of assistants and overworked.

It is not possible to mention H. C. Stewart without commenting on his amazing range of talents. Apart from being Director of Music, he played cricket for Kent 71 times; was reserve for the Oxford Boat; was an outstanding soccer player and an international-class ice-skater; won the Tonbridge Town tennis singles for many years, and was almost unbeatable at billiards. Can you imagine our present musicians doing just one of these? He was also charming and modest!

The sport on offer was quite varied. The 1st XI played a large variety of clubs, though there were still few school matches. A letter to *The Tonbridgian* complains because school teams playing away have to pay their own expenses. The first cross-country race was held against South London Harriers in 1909. One OT, H. E. Holding, ran for England in the Olympics half-mile in 1908 and another, C. C. G. Wright, later to become a master, was winning his fourteenth rugby cap for England. Unfortunately fixtures were frequently disrupted by epidemics. In his Skinners' Day speech the Master of the Skinners promised a new sanatorium and a new organ for the chapel, as the present one was suffering from asthma.

1908 saw the retirement of one of the keenest supporters of Tonbridge sport, Henry Hilary. Appointed Head of Mathematics by Welldon in 1870, several of his former pupils became wranglers; he was also a classical scholar and an expert in Oriental languages and Arabic. He was offered and refused the Chair of Chinese at Oxford, preferring to spend his life doing what he did best, teaching Maths and playing and watching cricket.

In 1909 the chapel was completed and the untidy temporary west end replaced by the spacious ante-chapel. At the same time the new organ, made by Binns of Leeds, was installed. The building, completed at a cost of £13,000 was dedicated by the Archbishop of Canterbury, Dr Davidson, assisted by two former Headmasters, Wood and Tancock. After the service, they immediately proceeded to the Shipbourne Road where the foundation stone of the new sanatorium was laid by the Bishop of Rochester.

The sanatorium just after it was opened in 1910. The ceremonial opening had to be cancelled because of the death of Edward VII. A boy patient moved in and it was open.

In the same year, Tonbridge received a royal visit from the Duke of Connaught, who came to inspect the Corps. In 1911 a contingent of the Corps went to London to take part in the Coronation procession. The entire Corps, by now about.300 in strength, went to Windsor Park to take part in the king's review, and it was announced in May 1911 that the school Shooting VIII had won the 'Schools of the Empire Cup' in 1910. In that pre-computer age the results of that competition, open to all schools in the Empire, took a year to work out.

In 1909 Arthur Lucas retired, and if one had to pick one master as being more important than any other, the choice would probably fall on him. Appointed by Rowe in 1878, Lucas founded Parkside and remained there almost until his retirement. He was Chaplain and manager of the School Mission. He was an enthusiastic cricketer and coach; he presented the cup for House cricket, and he organized the first cricket tour to Holland. He also started several school societies. He was the chief advocate of the new sanatorium. His wife was one of those ladies who contribute so much to her husband's success, and she organized Tonbridge support for the Melanesian Mission. She also cared for all the chapel vessels, vestments and flowers. As a couple they engendered great affection.

Lucas's place at Parkside was taken by R. L. Aston, a famous Old Boy and rugger international, who was to coach several successful school XVs. Aston was on the England selection committee and forced it to recognize the emergence of the specialist back row forward in the person of Charles Pillman (OT), who won fourteen England caps.

The years leading up to the War were relatively uneventful, apart from various sporting achievements by boys and Old Boys. K. L. Hutchings was playing cricket for England; C. H. Pillman and A. L. Heniker-Gotley followed Wright into the England XV, making 16 internationals since 1870. 'Gotley was the greatest of them all,' an OT wrote recently, 'but he emigrated!'

At school the first of the remarkable Knott brothers, F. H. Knott, was breaking all the cricket records. The four Knott brothers were the sons of the Revd. F. G. Knott, the first Headmaster of the new Skinners' School at Tunbridge Wells. In 1910 F. H. Knott scored 1,126 runs in school matches at an average of 80.43 – a record which was to last for 75 years. In 1912 the 1st XV beat all four of its school opponents, Dulwich, Sherborne, Uppingham and St Paul's, yet letters to *The Tonbridgian* complain of lack of school support at matches and ask why scientists are excused gym. In any case beating all four school opponents would not be possible again for many years because there was an almighty row with Dulwich which led to the abandonment of the fixture. The 1st XI scored 433 for 6 against Sherborne, and F. N. Sherwell scored 286 in the final house match.

The first reported death of an OT in a flying accident told the sad story of E. V. B. Fisher, aged 74, an aeronautical mechanic, who loved experimenting. *The Tonbridgian* records that he always wore his muffler when flying and had made one experiment too many. The lives of two

Skinners' Day, 1914; boys on way back from parish church. Until 1890 the boys had to attend the parish church on Sundays, but from Dr Wood's time attendance at the church was reduced to one service a year, on Skinners' Day. With the recent reduction in the seating capacity of the church even this service has had to be replaced with one in the school chapel.

A page from the book of photos of those who fell in the Great War. There were four Sherwell brothers at Tonbridge, all of them in the 1st XI. Rex Sherwell made 69 for the Lords Schools v. The Rest in 1914. He was shot down in France in 1916, at the age of 18, only a few days after he had escaped unhurt from another shot-down aircraft. Stokoe devoted one whole page to his short career.

boys were saved at the new sanatorium, and the first house singing competition was held. One OT, E. W. Nelson, was in the party which found Captain Scott's body, and a young OT, A. G. W. Warren, the best rackets player we had had till then, was killed playing rugger.

Just before the War, the Governors bought more playing-fields and land near the school, purchases which were to prove immensely beneficial. They bought the large field known as Martin's and removed the hedge which divided it from Le Flemings. They also bought Potkiln Farm, destined, many years later, to be the site of the vast expansion of sporting facilities which is still continuing. Between 1910 and 1919 they bought Parkside, Manor House, Judde House and Ferox Hall, taking all the boarding-houses out of private ownership, except Park House and Hill Side. The housemaster of Hill Side, E. C. Goldberg, suddenly died in 1915, and H. S. Vere Hodge took over. Goldberg was Head of Modern Languages and introduced Russian to the curriculum.

At this stage in Lowry's career it would seem that all was going well, and that he was providing the drive and vigour the school needed, but events on the world stage were about to ruin everything. A man steeped in Victorian ideals and Etonian tradition, he came to Tonbridge to put them into practice, only to have his earlier years overshadowed by the threat of war and his hopes shattered by the realities and tragedy of what was to come.

The last event of significance, one week before the War started, was the first match against Clifton at Lords. It is not possible now to be sure why Tonbridge and Clifton were invited to join the select group of Lords schools, but it was a deeply felt honour, which was to last until 1968 and cause more than a little jealousy among those schools not chosen. It was sad that the first match at Lords resulted in a crushing defeat.

Within a week, the War had started. By the time the boys returned in September 1914, several of the July leavers and some boys due to return had joined up, as well as three masters. Numbers dropped from 413 in July 1914 to 374 in 1916, but thereafter they recovered steadily. *The Tonbridgian* says surprisingly little about the early years of the War, but later, reduced in size, it became a catalogue of those killed and wounded.

To go into detail about casualties would be both depressing and exhausting. To pass over them would be disrespectful. The school has the benefit of one of the most comprehensive books possible on the subject.

H. R. Stokoe issued at intervals lists of those Old Boys and masters serving and those killed or wounded, and at the end of the War produced the lists in book form, with obituaries and photographs in almost all cases of those killed. The book was called *Tonbridge School and the Great War* and among those listed was Stokoe's own son. Altogether 2,382 boys and 21 masters and ex-masters served; 415 boys and three masters died. One VC, 86 DSOs, and 40 MCs were awarded to OTs and masters. Stokoe's book is one of the most thorough and painful records of the Great War ever compiled by any institution.

Just a few of those who died must be mentioned, without meaning any disrespect to the hundreds of others who gave their lives. Three of the most promising young masters died – A. H. Simpson, A. F. Botham and H. A. Hodges. Simpson, a young Science master, threw himself into all areas of school life, particularly the Corps, and the School Mission in St Pancras. He was the first master to join up, but died of pneumonia before he reached the front. Botham, a wrangler at Cambridge and captain of his college XV had been on the staff for only one year when he joined up, to be killed in action in 1917. Capt. H. A. Hodges had come to Tonbridge in 1909. At Sedbergh under Lowry he was captain of the XI for three years and of the XV for two. He was captain of the XV at Oxford and won international caps in 1906. He came to Tonbridge to run the rugger, and was a popular tutor of School House. He was twice mentioned in despatches and died in circumstances of exceptional bravery. One can only imagine how much the news of his death must have affected Lowry.

Old Boys who died included P. D. Kendall, a former England rugger captain, K. L. Hutchings, the England cricketer and Major Eric Dougall, who was awarded the VC on 10 April 1918, for leading his battery near Messines with conspicuous bravery and was killed in action four days later.

A War Memorial Fund was set up to pay for both a permanent memorial after the War and the funding of the education at the school of the sons of those killed or disabled. OT casualties at Gallipoli were particularly heavy.

In 1915 Rupert Croft-Cooke joined the school as a very young day boy. He stayed for only two years, but was later to achieve some fame as a novelist. His book *The Altar in the Loft* makes interesting reading. Some no doubt hate his rude comments about several masters, and as a day boy he seemed to devote much of his time to getting out of doing things, but at heart he seems to have liked the school, and some of his descriptive writing gives a genuine insight into the atmosphere of the school and town at that time. In 1917 S. P. B. Mais joined the staff for two years and later wrote at length about his time here in his book *All the Days of my Life*. He is very complimentary about Mr Lowry and Mr Earl and appreciative of his experiences at Tonbridge before he went off to Cranwell as a lecturer.

At school, as the War dragged on, work and sport continued very much as before, except that morning corps parades and daily PT sessions were added to the programme and different fixtures were played. Vegetables were grown on several playing-fields, and extra weeks' holiday granted so

Tonbridge School and the Great War by H. R. Stokoe. H. R. Stokoe, Housemaster of Park House, spent many years collecting details of all those who fell and all those who served in the Great War. 2,382 OTs and 21 masters served: 3 masters and 415 OTs died, including Stokoe's own son. Stokoe collected and reproduced photos of 401 of those who fell. For many years these were hung in the Memorial Corridor, and now they have been bound in a beautiful book which lies alongside this copy of Stokoe's book in a case in the Quad Chapel. The pages are turned regularly.

71

General French addressing the Corps after inspecting it in 1917.

boys could help at agricultural camps. As Mais says, the hum of German aeroplanes overhead and the sound of guns from Flanders acted as a permanent reminder, as well as the experience of hearing Lowry read out the long list of casualties. In 1917 General French came to inspect the Corps.

In 1917 Lowry's health broke down and he was ordered to rest. His problems must have been quite overwhelming. Not only did he have the triple burden of hearing news of the deaths of Old Boys from Eton and Sedbergh as well as Tonbridge, but masters to replace those on service must have been extremely hard to find. Trying to plan lessons and the curriculum became almost impossible, and there were the inevitable shortages of food and deterioration of the buildings to worry about.

In 1917 Alfred Earl was appointed acting Headmaster, and after Lowry's

Julius Caesar. Hoffy Arnold's Shakesperian productions were legendary, not least because he did not believe in scenery, which he thought detracted from the acting.

72

unexpected return in 1918, Earl retired. After Lucas he had probably contributed most to the school in his 34 years. He created a thriving Science Department; he supervised the building and running of the gymnasium; he founded Ferox Hall and was housemaster for 26 years. He was not popular with the other housemasters, however, because he had his own prospectus printed for Ferox, and was not above diverting boys to his house, where the food was better and the fees were higher.

In 1918 the Armistice was greeted with jubilation, and the celebrations, parades and processions are described in great detail in Rivington. Once the euphoria was over, however, the school, like every other institution in the country, was faced with a different world. In some areas it was possible to pick up the pieces; but in many a new start was needed, new faces, new methods, new ideas. Lowry and several of his staff were too old and too tired, but at least such men could set in motion the double task of re-establishing the school and making certain that those who had fallen were not forgotten. In 1919 a memorial service was held, and the Memorial Committee set about deciding on a permanent memorial. Surprisingly, Herbert Baker, the eminent OT architect, who was invited to design the Winchester and Harrow war memorials, was not invited to build the Tonbridge one.

Soon masters returned from the front, Gemmell and Arnold with MCs, and others retired or left. G. A. Floyd died in 1922. A popular and devoted master, he ran the tuck-shop. He left money for the Pavilion clock and for English prizes. The Corps sing-song included a jazz band for the first time. Old fixtures were renewed and the 1st XI entered a long purple patch, mainly thanks to cricketers of the ability of L. P. Hedges and C. H. Knott. *The Tonbridgian* printed a letter from an OT complaining that the post-war boys were scruffy, and an editorial on the problems of Sinn Fein and the Coal Strike. *HMS Pinafore* was performed in Big School, and, on a sadder note, Lt.-Cdr. Gaimes was in command of the submarine K5, which was lost off the Scilly Isles with all hands in 1921. An OT Dinner was held in Australia, and *Julius Caesar* was produced by Arnold, who was to produce so many Shakespeare plays with the assistance of his great friend Clemence Dane, the authoress, who visited the school frequently and wrote the words of two of the best-known school songs. H. C. Stewart returned to Oxford as organist at his old college, Magdalen, and was replaced by Dr T. Wood – Tommy Wood – an extremely talented musician and intriguing personality. In 1922 Gilbert Hoole joined the staff and, asked what he thought of Tonbridge in 1922, replied, 'I had the feeling that the school was trying to put the clock back to 1913!'

Some things certainly had not changed. Cricket and rugger dominated the pages of *The Tonbridgian*, and not without reason. Hedges scored 176 and C. H. Knott 220 in a partnership of 290 against Lancing, including 230 in an hour, out of a score of 520. Against Westminster, Hedges scored 193 and Knott 107 and the score at lunch was 306 for 3. There is a story that the Headmaster of Westminster went into the pavilion at 1 o'clock and saw

House Football Fifteen

A. T. Young (scrum) (Capt.) H. H. B. Gill f.
T. E. S. Francis (fly) F. C. Panckridge f.
V. Armistead f. F. A. A. Atkinson f.
E. Hammerling ¾ C. Marks ¾
D. C. Munro ¾ T. W. Whiler ¾
W. R. S. Panckridge f. G. A. Nicoll ¾
R. H. Kemsley f. G. C. Sumner f.
T. L. Shipman back

v. Judde House — won — 29–0
v. Manor House — won — 35–0
v. Day Boys A. — won — 35–3
v. Park House — won — 27–0 (Final)

FEROX HALL WON THE CUP
FOR THE FIRST TIME

The Ferox Hall House XV, 1919. A. T. Young and T. E. S. Francis entered Ferox Hall in successive years, 1916–17. They played together in the Ferox Hall, Tonbridge, Cambridge, and England XVs, usually as half-back partners. This is a copy of the team sheet in the Ferox Hall house annals.

Hedges fiddling with his pads. 'Hello, Hedges, I've come to watch you bat. Are you just going in?' 'I'm afraid I'm out, Sir.' 'Oh, bad luck, I'm so sorry! How many did you get?' '193, Sir.' E. W. Swanton reckoned it was the best schoolboy partnership ever. *The Times* congratulated the Westminster wicket-keeper on letting through only one bye in an innings of 486, and many years later that gentleman wrote to the *Telegraph*, saying that the ball only passed the bat once, and he was so amazed, he missed it. In 1919 the XI got their revenge at Lords by beating Clifton by 9 wickets. In 1920 E. P. Solbe scored 196 against Westminster and C. H. Knott had house match innings of 244, 103 and 372. In the final he put on 200 for the last wicket. Against Clifton he took 6 for 83 and 7 for 27.

In 1920 the XV beat Sherborne 34–0, Haileybury 33–0, and Uppingham 21–8. Dulwich and Tonbridge were still not speaking. In 1921 H. C. A. Gaunt, later Headmaster of Malvern, scored 960 runs, T. E. S. Francis 886, N. B. Sherwell 577 and J. C. Hubbard 528, a remarkable quartet for one season. For those who dislike sport, or sporting statistics, this section might be anathema, but never again was the school to produce so many stars at once. It is possible to assume that nothing else but sport mattered, and one's heart bleeds for the vast number of boys who passed through the school at this time uncapped, unheralded and unrecorded.

Yet at this very time and over the next few years a remarkable number of highly able boys entered the school, all to make their mark later in their own field. Croft-Cooke maintained that Tonbridge was a hot-bed of mediocrity, filled with the sons of accountants and stockbrokers, like himself. He was right in so far as we have produced few men of world fame or Churchillian achievement, but all through these early years of the twentieth century, a steady stream of talented boys graced the school with their presence.

In 1922 Lowry finally felt obliged to retire on health grounds. There was a short interregnum under Stokoe, though Gordon was the effective leader. Lowry died soon after he retired, at the end of 1922. He was a marvellous man; he had a great impact on Tonbridge, but the problems almost destroyed him. His obituary notices were understandably fulsome, as is shown in this short extract from *The Times*: 'Few schoolmasters of his generation had so wide and varied an experience; few have been better known; none has been better or more universally loved.'

Below. *Skinners' Day, 1920s; boys marching along the river.*

Below right. *Skinners' Day, 1920; boys being addressed by Mr Lowry.*

10

HAROLD SLOMAN

The Skinners have granted the School a gramophone, and a 'School' model of His Master's Voice Co. has been purchased. Records have also been given. Recitals take place on Tuesdays and Saturdays in Mr Dodd's Drawing School.

The Tonbridgian: *notice, 1923*

When Lowry announced his resignation, the Senior Classical Master W. M. Gordon, housemaster of Judde House, was persuaded to apply for the post, and with his long experience he was a very strong candidate. To his credit, many members of the Common Room hoped that he would be appointed Headmaster, and he was on a final short list of three, interviewed at Skinners' Hall. The Governors who had never quite got over Tommy Roots, their last inside appointment, in 1668, had their own reasons for not appointing Gordon and decided to appoint one of the outsiders – H. N. P. Sloman.

Harold Sloman was born in 1885. He won a scholarship to Rugby, where he was in the 1st XI and 1st XV. From there he won a classical scholarship to Balliol, where he obtained firsts in Greats and Mods., and in 1908 he went to Radley, where he was appointed master of the VIth form. In 1912 he was appointed Headmaster of Sydney Grammar School.

H. N. P. Sloman, by Kenneth Hauff (OT).

He had been in Australia a year when the War broke out, and he decided he must join the Army. The Australian Army refused to accept him on medical grounds, so, in 1916, he persuaded his Governors to give him leave to return to England to join the British Army. He was commissioned in the Rifle Brigade and went to Flanders, where he was wounded at Ypres and awarded the MC. He did not return to Sydney until 1919, and in 1920 he resigned because of his wife's health. In 1921 he became Head of the Modern Side at Rugby and in 1922 Headmaster of Tonbridge. He was the first Headmaster to have seen active service since Christopher Wase in the seventeenth century.

If the school was trying subconsciously to put the clock back to pre-war days, what it needed was a young man of varied talents to guide it into the uncharted waters of the post-war period. Sloman's war record and overseas

1st XV v. *Uppingham in 1923. There are many pictures of matches on the Fifty. They all look alike except for the trousers. With the recent sale of the Fifty they may become collectors' items – the photos that is.*

Mr Goggs opening the Pattison Rugger Pavilion in 1923. Unfortunately the Pattison Pavilion will be pulled down when the Fifty is vacated.

experience also appealed to the Governors. Somervell is very complimentary to him: Sloman, he says, was the most intellectually gifted Headmaster so far. He was an expert classicist, also able to teach VIth-form French and German. He was a gifted teacher, especially of clever boys. A competent cricketer and rugger player, he was also a keen rackets player and a mountaineer.

Gilbert Hoole, who joined the staff at the same time as Sloman, while agreeing up to a point with Somervell's comments, goes into more detail: 'Sloman came regularly into the Common Room during break, sat on the club fender and was always one of us. He was friendly towards junior masters. He was a clubable man who never seemed to be the Headmaster and never talked about school matters. A favourite expression was "not my pigeon", meaning "I leave it to you".'

Was this type of man the leader Tonbridge needed to pull it out of the past and steer it into the troubled 1920s and 1930s? The answer, weak as it is, seems to be 'yes' and 'no'.

At this particular point the task of a historian becomes more difficult because the last edition of Rivington's history was published in 1925, and Somervell's 1947 history skips over the last twenty years. However, many of Sloman's ex-pupils survive, as do two of his ex-masters. Some of their views collected and expressed here are complimentary, some not: and with his descendants still living it is not proper to be too specific, but it is such an important and long period in the school's development that it needs to be put in its right context. It is a complex story and it makes sense to do it chronologically.

The numerous buildings erected and land purchased in the previous 35 years had put a severe strain on the foundation, but the falling in of London leases and increased rents at the time enabled the Governors to consider providing some of those facilities which were still missing, and the period from 1923 to 1939 saw a steady building programme, assisted by a very good direct labour staff, under Mr R. Werren.

In 1923 the erection of the rugger pavilion on the Fifty, which had been

planned before the War, was finally possible, though this was done by appeal. It was built as a tribute to W. B. Pattisson, who had been in the 1st XI and the 1st XIII, 1869–70, and had died in 1913. His mother, Mrs Pattisson, a widow, used to live at Graylings, now the bursary, almost next door to the Headmaster's house. She had seven daughters and ten sons, seven of whom went to Tonbridge, and one of whom, R. M. Pattisson, played rugger for England. W. B. Pattisson was the fifth son and only managed to play cricket for Kent. The pavilion was built by private subscription and opened by E. H. Goggs, then in his eighty-eighth year.

Four tennis-courts were laid alongside the Fifty, and tennis matches were started. To the disgust of many die-hards, hockey received official recognition, with the awarding of 1st XI colours. Francis and Young were in the Cambridge XV, continuing the partnership they had begun in the Ferox Hall XV and the Tonbridge XV, and were to maintain until they played for the England XV together in 1926.

The first year of Sloman's reign was marred by the deaths in quick succession of three former Headmasters, Mr Lowry, Dr Tancock and Dr Wood, to all of whom tribute has been paid in earlier chapters, and in 1923 the school suffered another severe loss when W. M. Gordon was appointed Headmaster of Wrekin, where he was to be outstandingly successful. He had been Lowry's right-hand man and one of those masters boys constantly talk about in later years. He was a brilliant teacher and a powerful housemaster of Judde House, and he is best remembered for the style of his handwriting which he taught his boys to imitate. There is a story that two officers in India only realized they were both OTs, when one saw the other's Gordonian handwriting.

The Governors presented the school with a gramophone, and recitals took place on Tuesdays and Saturdays in the Drawing School. Dancing classes were introduced and no doubt regarded as a novelty by those unaware that dancing used to be part of the nineteenth-century curriculum. The school was allowed to go down town to the theatre: 'On Monday, February 5th, any of the School who wished were allowed to go down to

Skinners' Day, 1923. Sloman, the new young headmaster, looking rather surprised.

77

The War Memorial was dedicated in 1925. Its main feature, apart from tablets containing the names of all those who had fallen, was a set of gates, seen closed in this picture.

Below. *The Sports have been taken seriously since 1859. Originally they were held on the Head, but later on Martin's as well. Perhaps someone can identify the competitors shown in this race and give it a date.*

the New Theatre and see the dress rehearsal of "Tilly of Bloomsbury". Needless to say the whole School went with a will.'

These miscellaneous items may seem quaint to us now, but they at least reflect a slight move away from the obsession with sport which had dominated the previous decade.

In 1924 the school finally received its own armorial bearings and the OT Society presented a huge banner to be flown on Speech Day, on OT Day, at Lords and on other important occasions. The War Memorial Fund was still attracting donations and much thought was devoted as to how to spend the money. The education of the sons of OTs who had been killed in the War was the chief priority, and a tangible memorial to the fallen was also planned. It was eventually decided to erect a beautiful pair of Gates of Remembrance at the entry to the chapel from the ante-chapel. The gates were made of bronze and represented duty and sacrifice. Alongside were the names of all those who had fallen. The whole structure was almost the width of the chapel and made of bronze, marble, alabaster and carved oak.

On 10 October 1925, the memorial was dedicated by Bishop Wakefield and unveiled by Maj.-Gen. Sir Edmund Ironside. In addition, the originals of the photos in Stokoe's book, of those who died, were placed in the ground-floor corridor, known thereafter as the Lower Memorial corridor. *The Tonbridgian* published an illustrated chapel supplement for the memorial service, containing detailed descriptions of the war memorial and all the windows and other decorations.

In 1924 Dr Wood left and returned to Oxford. Tommy Wood was a remarkable man. His father had been a sea captain, and Tommy had been round the world before he joined the staff. Although he suffered from appalling eyesight, he insisted on joining the Corps as a cadet and parading with the boys and eventually he was promoted lance-corporal. He was a great popularizer of music and could write good tunes. He had already written the music to Clemence Dane's school song 'Hail and Farewell', one phrase of which forms the title of this book, and later he was to publish the *Tonbridge School Song Book* containing all the Tonbridge school songs and write the music for Vere Hodge's school hymn.

Sport seems to figure much less in *The Tonbridgian* at this time, though Arthur Young won the first of his eighteen England caps in 1924, and A. G. G. Marshall was selected for the Olympic team in Paris. In 1925 the OT Golf Society was founded under the presidency of General Ironside, with the express intention of entering for the Halford Hewitt Competition. *The Tonbridgian* pleaded for a Common Room play, and in his 1924 Skinners' Day speech Sloman said he wanted to see dramatic societies in every house. That evening Messrs. Bathurst and Staveley began their amazing partnership in the Gilbert and Sullivan productions that was to last for nearly 30 years.

On Skinners' Day 1925, Sloman announced that a day boy, Leslie Rowan, would be the next Captain of the School. He would not be the first day-boy Head Boy, but such an appointment was rare, and Sloman said it proved that boarders and day boys were equal. This was not yet the general view. 'Did you suffer from being a day boy?' I recently asked an ex-member of Day boys 'B'. 'Yes, terribly!' 'What form did the treatment take? Was it bullying, mental, physical or what?' 'We were just ignored!' The truth is that the day-boys' accommodation was limited and squalid: the praes of both day-boy houses shared a single room in Old Judde. 'It was like a ghetto,' my informant added.

The Tonbridgian mentions the looming political crisis only briefly. There is a single reference to the General Strike, but the editors say rather arrogantly that politics is not their concern. C. T. Tattershall Dodd Jnr. retired after teaching drawing to the Lower School for 24 years. His father had taught drawing for 11 years in the mid-nineteenth century. The younger TD was a martyr. Stories about what happened in his lessons are legion. As Sloman said in his farewell tribute at the OT Dinner: 'Mr Buckmaster taught those who wanted to learn drawing and Mr Dodd those who didn't. The fact that many of the latter went on to Mr Buckmaster is a tribute to Mr Dodd's patience.' One of the Art Department's old pupils, Herbert Baker, was knighted for his services to architecture, including designing public buildings in Delhi and South Africa. At the same OT Dinner Rowan was able to inform the Old Boys that the school had won all its school rugger and cricket matches.

In 1927 Old Judde was turned into a class-room block and Dry Hill House bought for the day boys. The two day-boy houses – natural antagonists – now faced each other across the corridor. Presumably the powers that be at Tonbridge or in London were unaware of boy politics. The new Music School was built beside the Avenue by the direct labour staff, and when it was opened, school music at long last had a building worthy of it. *The Tonbridgian* was enthusiastic: 'No more will the strains of cornet, flute, harp, saxophone and psaltery mingle with the effluvia produced by the untiring effort of our eminent scientists.'

The mid-1920s saw the appearance of two enterprising independent magazines – *Myops* and *Phoenix* – which were evidence of a vigorous intellectual movement in the school. They were well produced, readable and good value. With 125 boys learning instruments, music was at last on the upgrade and so was drama under Hoffy Arnold. In 1926 H. F. Ellis, Tonbridge's greatest humorist, had played Polonius in *Hamlet* and in 1928 Arnold's production of *King Lear*, with Alec Hill and Humphrey Tilling in the leading roles, brought rave reviews. Both were to figure again in the school's history in later life, one as a Governor, the other as President of the OT Society. The rackets pair reached the semi-final at Queen's – the furthest yet – and the 1st IV, coached by Tom Staveley, won the Public Schools IVs at Marlow. In 1929 sporting triumphs were quite varied, and the good old days seemed to be returning. P. Johnson won a rowing blue and a fellowship at Oxford at the same time, and the XI beat Clifton at Lords with 4 byes off the last ball.

The tuck-shop and Avenue in 1924. The tuck-shop is now the school shop and the Chestnut Avenue had to be pulled down in 1958 as it was dangerous.

Up to this half-way mark in Sloman's time, the school seems to have been doing well, and the list of activities certainly shows a widening of interests compared with pre-war times. Whether it was a better school because of it is difficult to tell. Day-to-day activities were still very much run by the praes, though it is not easy to tell if the boys were happy or if some found the boarding-school atmosphere oppressive. Reports received on those days are surprisingly conflicting.

The academic standard of the school raises some questions: the number of Oxford and Cambridge scholarships in this period was well down on pre-war figures because there was much greater competition from some very good grammar schools. Though Sloman had introduced the School and Higher Certificates, which provided much better yardsticks by which to measure a boy's achievements, and the VIth form contained some very able boys, the feeling is that the school was bottom-heavy – too many came without any hope of rising above School Certificate level and were lost in the murky regions of the Army class. However, numbers at the school were still at their peak and, if Sloman's regime lacked leadership, as has been claimed, life seems to have been busier and more varied than it had been in the past.

Indeed in 1930 *The Tonbridgian* complained that the Easter term was too full of competitions – Literature, Reading, Essay and Divinity prizes on top of the ever-expanding sports programme. The Easter term was frequently ruined by epidemics, and in 1930 the San Matron, Miss Phillips, died from pneumonia caused by exhaustion in caring for her patients. On Skinners' Day the Governors arrived in petrol-driven vehicles for the first time – a far remove from the horseback days of old. The library was on the move again, this time to Old Big School, and it was found that it contained 6,580 books. Somervell, the librarian, wrote in *The Tonbridgian*: 'There is no doubt the books have done more good to the boys than the boys have done harm to the books!' The first film ever shown in Big School was appropriately entitled *Rugger* – a suitable subject in a year which saw the death of R. L. Aston. An Old Tonbridgian Masonic Lodge had been formed in 1920, and Sloman, a keen Mason, was Master of the Lodge in 1931, when the Public School Lodges Festival was held at Tonbridge. Sloman delivered a short address on the history of the school to those attending.

In 1931 Toddy Goggs died at the grand age of 95. He left generous legacies to the games fund, the library and the war memorial fund. He also left £200 for history prizes, which has meant generations of boys having to work hard in the Easter holidays ever since. Stokoe retired after 41 years, and his dedication to the school and the OTs was legendary. His word was law in the Lower School: no boy could move to the Upper School without a qualifying spell in Stokoe's form – and some of his pupils found him rather stern.

An American magazine, reviewing *The Tonbridgian*, which it took regularly, came to the conclusion that OT must mean 'Old Timer'. At

L. P. Hedges, one of the greatest schoolboy cricketers of his time, who later played for Oxford University, Kent and Gloucestershire, died in 1933 at the age of 32.

80

sport a long bad patch was beginning, and 1931 was a year of excuses: the 1st IV caught a crab in the first race at Marlow. The other teams suffered from epidemics, injuries, rotten luck, bad refereeing etc. There were, however, some interesting developments: a scout troop was formed and a careers advisory committee established. Old Boys were asked for help with careers. The chapel had its first microphone, and, in 1932, 24 German boys came to spend a period at Tonbridge. The day-boy houses were renamed Welldon House and Smythe House, thus eliminating the derogatory nicknames Day bugs 'A' and Day bugs 'B'.

In 1933 J. C. Roper (OT) was appointed Archbishop of Ottawa. Later the school was shocked by the early deaths of two of the greatest OT games players, I. P. Hedges and A. T. Young. Hedges had never quite fulfilled the promise he showed at Tonbridge and Oxford; Young had won 18 caps for England – a good number in those days. Francis meanwhile had emigrated to South Africa. The cricket and rugger results no longer reflected the glory of the early 1920s. R. W. M. Morrison of Park House won the cricket house matches single-handed, so that the OT newsletter says the House Match final was between Morrison and School House, and Morrison won. A year later Rowan and Morrison played against each other in the England v. Scotland hockey match. R. S. Haines played hockey for Ireland, while J. C. Hubbard had played rugger for England in 1930 and W. G. S. Johnston for Scotland in 1935 and 1937. So much for Tonbridge being parochial! But the big feats of 1934 were performed by J. G. W. Davies. In the same season, playing for Cambridge, he took eight wickets in the Varsity match and, against the Australians, bowled Don Bradman for a duck. He has never lived it down. In 1933 *The Tonbridgian* contained an account of the old game 'Stumper' which had been so popular many years earlier.

In 1933 the old Skinners' Day tradition of the whole school going to the swimming-pool before breakfast was abandoned. For many years, it had been traditional for the Head Boy to dive into the river followed by the whole school, then march to the Rose and Crown to shout for the Master of the Skinners to come out on the balcony in his dressing-gown and address them. When the river became too insanitary, the pool was used instead. Unfortunately this had led, in previous years, to town v. gown hostility and rowdiness. The depositing of a milk-float in the swimming-pool probably precipitated the demise of this tradition, which was linked to the birch boughs which still adorn the school on Skinners' Day. There has been much disagreement about the origin of this custom, though it would seem to be associated with old May Day traditions rather than having any disciplinary significance.

In 1934 the first school dance was held in aid of the Tonbridge clubs. This event was to be very popular for the next 30 years, and boys went to great lengths to decorate Big School. Some very interesting photos survive of these early dances.

In 1936 the Biology and Art departments were moved to a new building

Above. *A. T. Young, who played rugger for England 18 times between 1924 and 1928, also died in 1933, at the age of 31.*

north of the chapel, enabling the Physics and Chemistry departments to expand. The new building was opened with due ceremony by the Duke of Kent. Further up the Avenue, beyond the Music School, a new 'Grubber' was opened – probably a building of more interest to the boys of those days than any of those just mentioned. All these buildings were built by the Works Department. The old fives- and squash-courts were pulled down and replaced by a block of four new squash-courts. A year later the OTs reached the final of the Londonderry Cup.

Gas masks arrived and a tear gas chamber was installed, but the Germans came back on another visit in 1937. The 1st XI lost to them 1–3 at hockey on the New, having had to stand while their opponents gave the 'Heil Hitler!' salute before the match: the visitors put on a show in Big School full of goose-steps and 'Heil Hitlers'. The 1st XI paid a return visit to Germany, and the way the OT Letter wished them well and hoped they wouldn't be arrested for not 'heiling' makes one wonder if the threat of war was taken seriously, even at that late stage.

By now numbers had started to decline seriously and rumour has it that there were behind-the-scenes moves by some Old Boys to persuade Sloman to go. The school had acquired a reputation for slackness, which the masters thought was unfair. The truth was that Sloman did not care or bother about public relations. He refused to flatter prep school headmasters, and he did not much like parents, especially stockbrokers.

Ironically in 1937 the school obtained more passes at School Certificate than any other school, and the sports results started to return to their old standard. OTs were prospering: G. A. Hill was appointed captain of the Walker Cup team; J. J. F. Pennink won the Amateur Championship twice and was also in the Walker Cup team; H. C. A. Gaunt, another famous games player, was appointed Headmaster of Malvern, and W. F. Oakeshott Headmaster of St Paul's.

At the OT dinner, the chairman, Sir Kaye Le Fleming, a famous surgeon, must have nonplussed Sloman by saying that he never learnt anything at school. In reply Sloman complained that he never saw the parents because they never came to school. In 1939, though still only 54, he resigned.

I will end by quoting one of his masters:

Sloman kept a low profile: under a competent if somewhat restless staff, the school pursued its quiet way. Sloman was no Crusader, no Captain Cook energetically seeking new territories to explore, no Darwin with revolutionary ideas to promote. He was more like the Captain of a Channel ferry, relying on his crew to keep the ship on its prescribed course.

It is significant that, as proof of their regard, the masters entertained Sloman to a farewell dinner, an event believed to be without precedent.

11

ERIC WHITWORTH

*One Headmaster sent me his good wishes and added that I was a
very brave man in taking over Tonbridge!*

E. E. A. Whitworth's Diary, 1939

Eric Whitworth was educated at Radley and won a classics exhibition to
Trinity College, Cambridge. After Cambridge, he joined the staff at
Rugby, served in the Army in the War, in which he won the MC, and
returned to Rugby where he became a housemaster. He was appointed
Headmaster of Bradfield in 1928, and in 1939 was appointed Headmaster of
Tonbridge at the age of 50.

Whitworth is the only Headmaster of recent times to leave a set of
memoirs to which we have access. It is not clear when they were written,
and occasionally the facts listed in them do not quite agree with records
obtained from elsewhere, but the value of such documents is incalculable.
At the beginning of his Tonbridge section he admits that he was afraid that
the Governors of Tonbridge might prefer a younger man, but, with his
brisk manner, military bearing and down-to-earth views, the Governors
obviously saw in him the man to put some backbone into the school.

*E. E. A. Whitworth, by
Edmund Nelson.*

They could not have made a better choice. As the memoirs show, he
gave considerable thought to the duties of a headmaster, and to the special
needs of his new school. He was appointed in April 1939, and in June, at a
meeting with the Governors, he was told that his chief concern must be to
restore good relations with the Old Tonbridgians and prep school
headmasters. He says quite openly that he had been warned to expect a
school riddled with slackness – one prep school headmaster even wrote to
him, commiserating with him and wishing him the best of luck.

Whitworth found that there were many questions about the school that
he wished to discuss with Sloman and finally invited him to lunch at his
London club. Sloman seemed deliberately to avoid talking about the
school, and Whitworth decided that Sloman was unaware of his
responsibility for the sharp decline in numbers. As they parted, Whitworth
asked Sloman to give him one piece of advice about Tonbridge. Sloman's

answer was to advise him to keep his white wine in London, because the School House cellars were only suitable for red wine. Whitworth regarded this as confirmation of what he had heard about Sloman. Those who knew Sloman, however, say that it sounds like a typical Sloman leg-pull.

During the summer holidays of 1939 Britain moved towards war. On 2 September Whitworth, surprisingly, was still on holiday in Devon with his family, and the housemasters were holding the fort at Tonbridge. Whitworth received a telegram from the school secretary, asking him to return at once, so he got into his car and drove back to Bradfield for the night. On 3 September he heard Chamberlain announce the outbreak of war on the radio, then drove to Tonbridge to take up residence in the Rose and Crown.

He immediately called a housemaster's meeting in the middle of the holidays and Somervell reports: 'I cannot forbear to say how greatly we were encouraged by the quiet confidence with which he faced the unknowable future of a school he had not yet begun to rule.'

So he set to work, confronted by the internal problems he had expected and an even greater batch of external problems caused by the outbreak of war. All headmasters must have faced the latter; few, if any, had to take up the reins of a new school on 3 September in a school right in the path of German aeroplanes.

His first and most pressing problem was the arrival of Dulwich College. He remembered that Sloman had vaguely mentioned Dulwich, but he discovered that they had started to evacuate on 1 September and that within a few weeks 615 boys and their masters would be descending on Tonbridge. He had an urgent meeting with W. R. Booth – the Headmaster of Dulwich – and they agreed to a plan to share class-room and playing-field accommodation. Tonbridge would follow their normal routine; Dulwich would have lessons in the early afternoons and evenings and games and recreation in the mornings. Whitworth felt that he had been less than generous to Booth but also felt that, to help cure Tonbridge's problems, he needed to see its normal routine in action for at least a term. Fifty Dulwich boarders were selected to fill the vacancies in the Tonbridge boarding-houses; the other boys were found lodgings in the town by the Dulwich staff.

For one term the arrangement worked as smoothly as could be expected, but, in December, Dulwich went home – to the relief of both schools. Naturally the annual rugger match on the Fifty in 1939 led to strong feeling, with a crowd reported to be 2,000.

The Governors, with considerable foresight, had used the lull since Munich to have large concrete shelters built for each boarding-house, equipped with benches for sleeping and electric light, but for the first two terms of the War there was little need to use them, and Whitworth was able to turn his attention to the more pressing internal problems of the school.

In September 1939, 30 boys had been withdrawn because of anxiety over the school's position in a danger zone, and term had started with numbers down to 376. Whitworth, aware of the need for more discipline, found an ally in the Head of School, Michael Lloyd, who told him that the praes would co-operate in any new rules he wished to introduce. By half-term he had decided on a few new rules – minor changes, but it would be a start – and the housemasters agreed to them. In future boys should remove their hands from their pockets as an act of courtesy when passing masters or their wives; leaves off would be more tightly controlled, and masters should wear gowns in class. The next term he had to take the painful decision to close Park House in April and transfer boys to other houses of their own choice. Lloyd chose to join him in School House.

After the evacuation of Dunkirk, Tonbridge town found itself embroiled, not only as a railway junction on the direct route from Dover, but also as a key defensive point astride the Medway. The town became a fortress, with most of the school inside the perimeter and most of the boarding-houses outside. An anti-tank trench was dug alongside the Head, and Major Dixon, the master who commanded the Corps, always boasted that he had persuaded the Army not to dig it right across the Head. The first serious air raids took place, and the alarm sounded repeatedly. For the summer term of 1940, which was very hot, the boys slept fitfully in the air-raid shelters and the masters at the door or just outside. Tonbridge was not a target however, and this practice was abandoned, just as the carrying of gas masks was later limited to boys having to carry them outside the school grounds or after lock-up – what Somervell calls a typical British compromise.

The geographical position of the school became even more dangerous because of the difficulty of dispersing the boys by road or rail in the event of an invasion. It happened that two OTs were in key military posts. Field Marshal Ironside was CIGS and Air Marshal Sholto Douglas was Assistant Chief of Air Staff. Whitworth started to plan for evacuation, but to his surprise, he confesses, Ironside, who had a son in the school, continued to attend Sunday morning chapel, in mufti, even during the early months of 1940. Whitworth appealed for help to other headmasters, but the only school to respond was St Edward's, Oxford, who generously offered to share their buildings. Whitworth and Hoole went to Oxford to make provisional arrangements, but these were never taken up.

Apart from this, the term progressed with surprisingly little disruption. In July 1940 Skinners' Day took place as usual, though there was an air-raid warning during the afternoon tea-parties. In his speech to the parents Whitworth paid tribute to Michael Lloyd, who was about to enter the RAF. He was to be killed in action in 1943. He also paid tribute to Messrs Buckmaster, Ridgeway and Churchyard, retiring after 114 years' service between them.

The school broke up two days early, but the 1st XI went to Lords as usual for their two-day match. Clifton, understandably, declined to travel to London, and Stowe accepted an invitation to take their place. Tonbridge won an exciting match, mainly thanks to a brilliant innings by their captain T. R. R. Wood, who scored 100 in an hour. His innings was described by some observers as 'the greatest schoolboy innings ever'. Sadly Wood was killed in the RAF in 1942.

The Headmaster of Shrewsbury then offered to receive the school and tentative plans were made to move. At Tonbridge some parents were very anxious to move. Numbers dropped again, not so much from boys being withdrawn as from new boys not being entered. Whitworth decided to hold a meeting of day-boy parents, who voted by a large majority for the school to stay put.

In his memoirs Whitworth records that he then went to see Ironside at his headquarters to ask his advice. Ironside had resigned as CIGS and been made C.-in-C. Home Forces. Ironside's instructions were: 'Have everything ready to go, but don't go; and if I have any reason to change my mind I will let you know.' The message never came.

After a spate of Luftwaffe bombing activity over southern England the school returned some days late on 1 October. On 20 October, Whitworth was walking by the river with his wife when they saw a lone German bomber approach the town and heard an explosion. Returning to school they found that the bomb had landed a few yards north of the chapel, causing very little damage but smashing some class-room windows. A few days later a British bomber crashed into some houses near the sanatorium, and its engine hit the outside wall, a few yards from the head of one of the patients. The school did not suffer any more damage from the air until 1944, but naturally such alarms did not inspire parents to enter their sons for the school, and it was an age of wild rumour. The Skinners' Company were already having to finance a large annual deficit, and the school properties in London suffered considerable damage; so serious did the threat of falling numbers become that the OT Newsletter for 1941 pleaded: 'Please announce that we have NOT been bombed!'

In August 1940 Flight-Lieut. E. J. B. Nicolson (DB 1930–4) was awarded the VC for the most conspicuous bravery shown in continuing to attack an enemy plane, even when his own plane was on fire.

During the autumn the raids on London intensified, and Sunday evening chapel was moved to the afternoon, as the chapel had no black-out. The immediate scare was over however, though considerable time and energy were devoted to ARP duties, with some masters serving as special con-stables and most boys and masters over 17 called up for the Home Guard.

It is usually assumed that casualties in the Second World War were far fewer than in the First, but Tonbridge lost 415 in the former and 297 in the latter, and Whitworth, like Lowry, had to bear the strain of hearing of the deaths of Old Boys from previous schools as well – Radley, Rugby and Bradfield. His memoirs for this period remain remarkably composed, giving the impression that they may have been written later, possibly after his retirement. However, he clearly relished the challenge, though the problems of obtaining good masters, good domestic staff, common entrance candidates and even school fixtures, must have been considerable.

Unabashed, he pressed on with his reforms. He was satisfied that the VIth form was being well taught; he felt he had particularly good VIth-form masters in Vere Hodge, Eames, Morris and C. B. Gordon, but he found that the standard of the Lower School was bad, and that masters were being slack about setting and marking prep. He introduced a system of fortnightly marks, form orders and reports, which a boy had to show to his housemaster. Much of this system is still in use. He made all boys study Divinity and persuaded far more masters to teach it, insisting on taking each of the VIth forms for Divinity himself. As housemaster of School House he leaned heavily on his house tutor   John Knott – but he and his wife always entertained boys to breakfast and supper on Sundays.

Each day he liked to walk round the school grounds visiting the games fields or the river, the gym and the sanatorium. If he happened to see some boy – the more junior the better – score a try, he made a note of it to be included in his end-of-term report. This went down splendidly with the parents. He was nearly always accompanied by his Irish setter, Paddy, which never seemed to come when called, and for which he bought one of those supersonic whistles, which did not work either. Usually he was dressed in his mac and his trilby, and one of the funniest sketches ever seen in the Corps sing-song was when a boy borrowed his mac, his hat, his whistle and his dog and persuaded it to cross the stage followed by the boy, looking for all the world like Whitworth, frantically and vainly blowing on the whistle.

This is enough of Whitworth as a man. He was an unqualified success. He had no pretensions, particularly academic ones. He was just a realist. A kind man, he looked severe and he could be firm. The sanatorium matron did not like the way he kept dropping in on the patients, so she did not stay long. He was quite prepared to sack boys, in spite of the low numbers, and he had some success in finding new staff, even in those difficult times. Two of his most successful appointments were Hervey Adams, the new Head of the Art Department, and Allan Bunney, the new Director of Music.

M. A. Buckmaster had been in charge of Art for 50 years, but he was only part-time, and depended on his assistants. Hervey Adams changed everything. The Art School was still quite new, and Hervey had unlimited enthusiasm. A marvellous painter himself, he inspired his pupils as well as introducing pottery and book-binding. He wrote books and broadcast on the teaching of Art. If you were lucky and had Art on Wednesday afternoons you could listen to the Derby on his radio, and if you had a French oral in the little exam room in the Art School, he was usually handy with a dictionary. He stayed for only 22 years, but he was a star. At first he irritated Whitworth by insisting on living out in the country so that he could paint; Whitworth forgave him when he discovered that Hervey's cottage was surrounded by blackberries, for the picking of which Whitworth had a passion.

The OT cricket team which played the Old Cliftonians in a POW camp in Germany in 1941. A team of eleven OTs played a team of eight Old Cliftonians at Biberach. Tall chairs were used for wickets, and a tennis ball and sawn-off pieces of wood for bats. After 4 balls the OTs were 0 runs for 4 wickets. They recovered to make 23, and the OCs were all out for 18. Later a German photographer took this photo of nine of the OT XI. When Brian Phillips sent the photo and the scores back to Tonbridge, he was so embarrassed by them he multiplied them by 10. The Tonbridgian printed the photo in 1942. Those shown are: I. Buckland, B. Gunnell, C. Willis, B. Phillips, C. Worrin, J. Lavington, J. Mertens, H. Plews, D. Bartlett.

Allan Bunney similarly transformed the Music department. He was at his best as a choir master and was particularly appreciated by those masters who sang in the choir. He re-established the orchestra, produced several organ and choral scholars, raised the Gilbert and Sullivan to new heights and bullied everyone into participating. He was probably Whitworth's most inspired appointment, though not without his moods. Whitworth was once seen fleeing down the Avenue during an air raid, looking unusually worried. He explained to another master as he passed that he was escaping from Dr Bunney.

He appointed Cecil Bullock, a graduate, to take over the gym. The unpopular morning PT sessions were replaced by weekly lessons in the gym for every class. With John Knott in charge of the cricket and rackets and James McNeill in charge of rugger, sport was the least of Whitworth's worries, though in the early days of the War few teams wanted to come to Kent, and the fixture list was subject to many changes. After a good cricket XI in 1940, Tonbridge teams during and just after the War went through a very long, lean patch. The drop in numbers must have contributed to this – at one time there were only about 110 boys over 16, and some games had to be taken by masters who were either elderly or unqualified. Still, all schools suffered from these problems, and it must be admitted that for a time we were just bad. One interesting excuse put forward for constantly losing to Uppingham and Haileybury at rugger was that East Anglian farmers had done well out of the War and sent their sons to those two schools; their forwards did look rather large and well-fed.

A large area of playing-fields here was turned over to vegetables and each house had its own allotment. Lyn Thomas, the Head of Biology and master in charge of tennis, proved a genius at producing vegetables with boy labour, though he probably did most of the labour himself. If the XV was no longer capable of beating Uppingham, at least the school produced 62 tons of potatoes and 17 tons of cabbages. Forty-six boys were trained as tractor-drivers by the daughter of the Dean of St Albans. In Whitworth's diary there is a photo of these boys being taught by this lady with a comment by his son – ('No wonder it was popular!') – and another photo in the same section shows boys weeding, with Ironside's son to the fore.

In 1941 H. R. Newgass (HS and DB 1913–17) was awarded one of the few George Crosses given during the War for defusing a land-mine which had fallen inside a gas-container in Liverpool. Had he not done so, the damage to the city would have been appalling.

By 1941 numbers had fallen to 306 – a drop of nearly 200 in four years – and *The Tonbridgian* was reduced to three very thin issues a year. Reluctantly Whitworth decided that Ferox Hall should close in December and its boys and housemaster transferred to Manor House, when Arnold, who had been housemaster for 22 years, retired. Arnold is one of those larger-than-life figures, a scientist who loved literature, drama, fine furniture and pictures and imparting his love of all these things to boys. In 1942 H. R. Stokoe died, leaving his marvellous book as a permanent tribute to his dedication to the school and Old Boys. Mr Campbell Jones, designer of the new buildings and the chapel, also retired after 50 years as architect of the Skinners' Company. He did not presumably design the notorious Ferox Hall cap of whose demise *The Tonbridgian* wrote: 'We welcome the disappearance of the ghastly coal-heaver's cap.'

Arnold's productions, which are now legendary but were staged against stark scenery, depended on good acting. Now, new stage-lighting and sound equipment were installed and Dickie Booth staged some memorable productions before he enlisted. In 1940 Eames and Foster started the Film Society which was to prove so popular on Saturday evenings.

The Tonbridgian reported that the OTs had played the Old Cliftonians at cricket in a POW camp. At this time the old iron-railings were removed from the front of the school to make munitions or saucepans. Rumour has it that they were never used, but they were never to reappear. The Avenue gates had been carefully hidden and did reappear after the War. Ferox Hall became an old people's home; Old Judde was taken over by the ARP and Dry Hill House by the Red Cross, so that the day boys lost their base. The Boat Club were given 48 hours' notice to vacate their club, as the Medway was to be designated a waterway of national importance. Anyone who knows that unprepossessing stretch of water will be amazed. In the event the Boat Club was reprieved. Soon after, the 1st IV was involved in a farcical race against Winchester at Windsor, when the organizers had overlooked the fact that it was Bank Holiday, and the Tonbridge crew had to avoid an oncoming tourist boat by steering into the bank. New equipment was not to be had in war time, but the Boat Club were much indebted to their old friends, the King's School, Canterbury, who lent us their oars when they evacuated to Cornwall. When King's returned from evacuation after the War and wanted their oars back, unfortunately there were hardly any left.

The first carol service of Seven Lessons was held, and the space under the organ was turned into a beautiful Lady Chapel. The Corps was inspected by General Montgomery, and in 1942 Air Marshal Sholto Douglas visited his old school. Whitworth took the first tentative steps to abolishing fagging, which incurred the predictable wrath of *The Tonbridgian*.

In 1943 Sidney Keyes, not yet 21, was killed in action. Many people consider him to be one of the two best poets of the Second World War. Tom Staveley, his English master, naturally thought he was the best. Keyes was grateful to Staveley for nurturing his talent and said that he found Tonbridge 'a civilized school, tolerant of those who preferred debate and writing to scrummaging'. By 1941 he was one of the leading poets of his generation. Staveley said of him: 'He had that rare hallmark of poetic genius, his capacity to hit the ear and eye at once with the impact of a single image.' One of his poems is included on the right.

In 1944 Wing Commander Nicolson VC was killed in the Far East. He had returned to duty after recovering from the severe burns received in his famous dog-fight. An article in *The Tonbridgian* many years later described

War Poet

I am the man who looked for peace
    and found
My own eyes barbed.
I am the man who groped for words
    and found
An arrow in my hand.
I am the builder whose firm walls
    surround
A slipping land.
When I grow sick or mad
Mock me not nor chain me:
When I reach for the wind
Cast me not down:
Though my face is a burnt book
And a wasted town.

Sidney Keyes

The War Memorial, 1939–45. The war memorials were almost the only parts of the chapel to survive the fire. The remains of the organ loft fell on them and protected them.

it thus: 'To other pilots it was a grotesque incongruous sight – a trim, near unmarked Messerschmitt chased by a blazing Hurricane.'

In June 1944 a V1 (buzz-bomb) landed near Ferox Hall. Considerable damage was done to the school, and many windows were broken. The only reported casualty was Whitworth, who was playing bridge in his drawing-room and was cut on the forehead. Meanwhile in London, Skinners' Hall was badly damaged by another buzz-bomb and Whitworth records that he did not like going to London to Governors' meetings much in those days. For the first time in memory, if not ever, Skinners' Day was cancelled, and the Lords match transferred to Clifton. However, prospects were improving. Numbers started to rise steadily and in September 1944, Park House reopened under Gilbert Hoole. Dr Bunney, ever full of new ideas, wrote a new tune for the traditional end-of-term hymn, 'Lord Dismiss Us' and the school went on strike and refused to sing it – the first signs of a post-war spirit? Of course Bunney maintained that within a few years boys would regard his tune as the traditional one, and he was proved absolutely right.

In March 1945 an extra Skinners' Day was held and on VE Day a large bonfire was lit in the anti-tank trench. In 1946 Ferox Hall reopened under James McNeill and the hideous water-tanks were removed from the front of the school. The OT cricket-, golf- and rackets-clubs resumed operations, and the first OT Dinner for seven years was held under the chairmanship of Lord Ironside, with a record attendance of 256. In 1946 numbers were up to 445 and the first rise in fees for many years was announced. Boarding fees rose from £142 to £170 and day-boy fees from £59 to £66. Whitworth was able to announce that he was raising the Common Entrance standard. During the War the school had suffered from his having to accept boys of almost any standard. He admitted it, saying 'They're perfectly nice chaps; they just haven't got any brains.' Meanwhile Dr W. R. Knightley left a large bequest to the Modern Language department. On 14 July a memorial service was held for the 297 OTs who died in the War, and stone tablets containing their names were erected next to the First War memorial panels.

In 1946 a new scheme for the school was introduced by the Minister of Education by which: 'The school is no longer to be called the Free Grammar School of Sir Andrew Judde, Knight, but simply Tonbridge School and is to be maintained as a secondary public school for boys as boarders, and, if the Governors think fit, as day boys.'

This seems to settle the argument about free education once and for all. Since then the day boys living within 10 miles of the school have also lost their right to a reduction in fees without a means test.

At the end of the War a Social Club was formed for the non-teaching staff. It gave them a greater sense of belonging to the school community, and was run by a committee who organized many enjoyable outings, dances, matches and so on.

In 1947 H. S. Vere Hodge, Head of the Classics Department, retired after 41 years. About this time the school hymn he had written, 'For him who dreamed of founding', with music by Tommy Wood, was introduced and has been sung with great pleasure by many generations since. He also left his house and land at High Trees to the Skinners' Company for the benefit of the school, which has turned out to be a very valuable bequest. Some other long-serving men also retired – Mr R. Werren, Clerk of Works for 47 years, Sgt.-Maj. Sturgess, the popular NCO, and Fitzgerald, bandmaster, head porter, and the man everyone went to when they wanted anything.

During Whitworth's remaining three years he was able to concentrate on less taxing matters. He introduced the annual 'Expedition Day' when boys were supposed to go off on trips of their own choosing. He appointed Logie Bruce Lockhart, the Scottish international, to take over the rugger from James McNeill, and he was as delighted as anyone that providence sent us two outstanding future games players, Colin Cowdrey and David Marques. Gradually, very gradually, the sport improved, though it never resumed its old predominance – there was too much else happening.

It is not possible to overestimate Whitworth's contribution to Tonbridge School. He said he would retire at 60 and, in 1949, he did, even though the Governors asked him to stay on. Three years after he died in 1971, the new day-boy house was named after him. In the Whitworth House dining-room there is a picture of him. The plaque beneath it says:

E. E. A. Whitworth MC, MA
Headmaster of Bradfield and Tonbridge
After whom this House was named
Regarded as one of the great Headmasters of Tonbridge

The 1st XI v. Old Tonbridgians, 1946. One of the earliest pictures of Colin Cowdrey – middle row, second from right.

12

LAWRENCE WADDY

I would rather a boy published a book of sonnets than win all the Lords matches going.

Lawrence Waddy, 1950

Lawrence Waddy, by John Ward.

For obvious reasons the appointment of the first post-war Headmaster in 1949 makes a suitable point to stop and reflect. The two wars are over, and the school is approaching its fourth centenary. This history is entering its final section, and the history of the last 40 years is in some ways the most difficult to tackle. On the one hand the two main sources of knowledge cease to help because the latest editions of Rivington and Somervell do not reach this date. *The Tonbridgian* also is less useful in so far as it becomes more pro-establishment and correspondingly more turgid. Contributors seem reluctant to express opinions. Consequently the historian becomes more dependent on his own experience and those of others, and they all say the same thing – that life in the last 40 years has become more frantic, more earnest, and it is harder to find much amusing to say. One hankers for the more leisurely days of Thomas Knox riding round the Head on his horse and the little boy going without his puddings.

Further, this last act of the drama is the hardest to describe fairly because many of the players or their dependants are still alive, and to hurt any of them would be unforgivable.

Thanks to the remarkable efforts of Whitworth and his staff the school had not only survived the War in better shape than might have been expected, but had come through the depressing post-war austerity period with numbers approaching their old peak, the entry lists full and a renewed faith in the future of public schools, in spite of the political threats being made at that time.

Everybody – Whitworth, Governors, staff – knew that a new vision was needed, and for months after Whitworth announced his retirement, there was lively discussion about what sort of man the Governors would appoint. Somervell, who was pessimistic about the future of public schools, for financial rather than political reasons, thought that a financier or lawyer was needed, and suggested either Jasper Rootham, an OT and a director of Lazards with a remarkable war record, or else E. Holroyd Pearce, a former Master of the Skinners' Company, and a brilliant lawyer, later to become Lord Pearce. Many other names were mentioned, but the Governors surprised everyone by appointing a young clergyman of 34, the Revd. Lawrence Waddy, a Chaplain of Winchester College.

Son of an Archdeacon, educated at Marlborough, a classical exhibitioner of Balliol, Lawrence Waddy had served as a naval chaplain during the war, before rejoining the staff at Winchester. He had the advantages of being young, handsome, lively and married to a young wife. He had the disadvantages of having had very little experience of schoolmastering and none at all of housemastering. Waddy was to spend 13 years at Tonbridge and his time as Headmaster has led to much debate, but before attempting to reach a fair and sensible assessment of his reign it is necessary to consider the state of the school when he took over.

In 1949 the fees were still very low, and Whitworth had not pleased everybody by insisting that they should remain so. Tonbridge had long had the reputation of being a good 'cheap' school, and such a reputation is not necessarily beneficial. Some masters hoped that a new Headmaster might come and put fees and salaries on a more realistic basis.

The curriculum was much as it had been before the War. Admittedly, in 1949, the standards in the Lower School were rising rapidly from their war-time low point, and Whitworth had been able to raise the Common Entrance level in his last few years, but there were still too many boys in the school who really had little hope of any academic achievement. To put it simply, the school was still bottom heavy. Also, although the Science side was rapidly becoming the biggest, it was still possible for an Arts boy to go through the school without a single science lesson, which did not make sense in this increasingly technical age.

Sport no longer held the predominant place at Tonbridge which it had before the War, but this was more through a succession of poor seasons than any policy imposed from above. For some reason the War had affected the sporting side of the school more seriously than might have been expected, and to the dismay of many older OTs, it took a long time to recover.

Finally, there still remained some of the worst elements of public school life of earlier days, crystallized in the complicated privilege system which still allowed boys to beat other boys and regarded the deliberate squashing of 'novi' as obligatory. This was very much worse in some houses, and OTs give remarkably different accounts of their early years at school in the 1940s and 1950s. Many boys liked the strict hierarchical system which operated, but many others were frightened by it and have never got over their aversion to it. These faults were prevalent then in most boarding schools of this type. Many people see them as an essential part of growing up and regard them as the good old days, but if there were defects in the system, then this was the time to change them.

Lawrence Waddy arrived in September 1949 – and here I must declare a personal interest. I happened, by good fortune and *faute de mieux*, to be Head of the School during Whitworth's last and Waddy's first terms. I was able to witness the difference between the two Headmasters at close quarters. My initial reaction to Waddy was, I think, fairly typical. While nearly all of us were totally devoted to Whitworth's memory and had nothing but good to say of the old man, we were excited by the prospect of this young ex-naval chaplain, about whom even the masters seemed to know nothing. Whitworth had always been proud of his 'open door' policy, but the fact is that Whitworth was rather awesome, and one always entered his study with some trepidation. When I rang Waddy's bell on the first day of his first term and waited outside the front door, I was astonished when the new Headmaster climbed through the floor-length window and greeted me with a slap on the shoulder.

He immediately set about getting to know us all. Supper and billiards, long walks, strange archaeological expeditions with him and his wife, Natalie, games of squash and rackets, cricket with the 1st XI, and a natural cheerfulness and modesty won many hearts among the senior boys. To most of us he was quite overwhelming. First impressions among the housemasters may not have been so favourable. He was, after all, younger than all of them, and it is probably true to say that he found it difficult to win them over. In addition, he was housemaster of School House, always the largest house, and whereas John Knott had been house tutor for 20 years, from 1944 onwards no house tutor ever remained at School House for long, which could not have made Waddy's job as housemaster easier. Tonbridge has always had house feeding, and the late 1940s was a difficult time because of rationing and for obtaining domestic staff; it must have been a daunting proposition for Natalie, a young mother and reserved by nature, to take on the burden of being a housemaster's wife, let alone a headmaster's wife.

Nevertheless, the scope offered to a new and vigorous headmaster was enormous, and Lawrence Waddy had more than just vigour to offer – he had astonishing versatility. In chapel his sermons were quite outstanding, and he was able to reinforce his belief in Christianity by appearing to be a man of simple and transparent faith. In addition he had a lovely speaking voice, which almost compelled people to listen. He was a good all-round games player, especially at hockey. He was a good classical scholar with a particular interest in Ancient History, and he was an excellent lecturer, talents he combined in his holiday duty as a lecturer on the Swan's Hellenic cruises to Greece and Turkey. His father had been Archdeacon of Jerusalem, which gave him an added interest in the Middle East. His real love, however, was drama, particularly religious drama, and he both produced house plays and wrote his own short religious dramas, some of them musicals, all of them moving.

He was a charitable man, and he believed in love. He certainly loved Tonbridge. Now, it is said, that Waddy arrived with a conviction that

The 1st XV of 1949 was possibly the best XV the school has had, winning all of its school matches. Both David Marques and Colin Cowdrey were in the team – middle row, second and fourth from left.

Tonbridge was too devoted to sport. Reading the school magazines of that period, it is probable that it no longer was, at least in the old way, though house cricket matches seemed to go on afternoon after afternoon, and the boys' games committee had almost as much power as the school praes. Waddy eventually got rid of the games committee, but before that he started the Athena Society, a society for VIth-form boys who held a termly dinner and discussion or lecture. This society was elective and élitist, which is what it was meant to be, and rather secretive, so it is not possible to say a great deal about it, but it did fulfil his wish to give a more intellectual tone to the Upper School.

However, no games player could ignore the presence of potential star performers of the calibre of Colin Cowdrey and David Marques, and they both became Heads of the School in his early years, entirely on merit. In Waddy's first term in 1949 the school had the best rugger XV it has possibly ever had, winning all its school matches, and both Marques and Cowdrey were in that team. However for several years after Waddy's first year the 1st XI and the 1st XV were not outstanding, and a predominance of sporting success could not have been one of his biggest problems. It was Waddy who reintroduced hockey as a school sport after a long gap.

The most pressing problem was to reconcile the standards and traditions of pre-war Tonbridge with a post-war society which, itself, did not know where it was going. Not only did the curriculum need a radical overhaul, but so did the complex structure of traditions and rules, many of them petty, which had taken a grip on Tonbridge for too long. To be fair to Waddy, one of the first things he did was to look at the written rules in the rule-book, known as the 'Memoranda' and in addition ask the school praes to list all the unwritten rules and privileges, both at school and house level. This was a complex task and we spent a long time on it. I was surprised, eight years later when I joined the staff, to find that little had changed. Some of the problems of the 1960s might have been avoided if a more vigorous pruning of outdated rules had happened in the 1950s. Some houses were much stricter than others, some praes were good, but several were not, and many boys of that decade still feel that they suffered from the system as it existed then and that Waddy could have done more to correct it. Possibly he wanted to but felt he did not have the support of the housemasters. One housemaster of that time says that they were willing to support him, but he did not make it easy, as boys discovered that they could go to him behind their housemaster's back. Perhaps he felt the school praes were doing a good job and did not wish to interfere.

A serious problem facing the school – or rather facing the Governors – was the eternal worry over finance. Fees had begun to rise, and the Governors took a conservative view over development. After the war years the finances needed a long period of consolidation. Possibly the Governors felt that the rapid expansion in the 20 years before the War had made Tonbridge one of the best-equipped schools in the country. Possibly the problems of building-licences, rising costs and uncertain birthrates gave them cold feet, but the only building planned during this period was the new South Wing extension opened in 1962, and even that was financed mainly by appeal.

On his first Skinners' Day in 1950, Waddy was able to announce that the school was full for years ahead and his first year had been a happy one. The curriculum had been amended in so far as Science was now part of the timetable for all boys in the IVth and Vth forms – the first major change in the curriculum for a long time. Fees were to rise to £200 p.a. for boarders and £90 p.a. for day boys. The Upper Hundred was regrassed to rescue it from its war-time damage, and Maurice Tate, the famous and much-loved England cricketer, was appointed cricket professional. Cowdrey made over a thousand runs in his last season and was chosen to play for Kent in the holidays; he also won the Public Schools' rackets singles. In his five years in the 1st XI he scored 2,894 runs at an average of 41.34 and took 216 wickets.

J. R. Thompson won the England amateur rackets singles, and the OT squash team of Phillips, Thompson, Curry, Rampton and Oliver won the Londonderry Cup for the first time. With a successful XV as well, Tonbridge sport was undergoing a revival, just at the time the new Headmaster was hoping to soften the image. He remarked wistfully that he would rather have one boy publish a book of sonnets than win all the Lords matches going. He was beside himself with glee when a 15-year-old Tonbridgian was invited to demonstrate his collection of armour on television. Two of us, both linguists, confronted with the depressing idea of spending 18 months doing National Service, went to him and, reminding him that he liked boys with original ideas, asked him if we could do our National Service in the French army, which we thought would be more useful. He thought for a minute, said that the only Frenchman he knew was Marshal de Lattre de Tassigny, the French C.-in-C. and that he was rather 'explosif', but he did know Montgomery and would see what he could do. Within a few days it was all fixed. The arrangement eventually fell through, but through no fault of either of them. Some of the letters are still in the archives. A minor episode, but it typifies his range of ideas and his eternal optimism.

G. L. Herman, the senior master, retired in 1949, and David Somervell in 1950, the latter to go to teach at Benenden. 'I'm going to be an Adam in a garden of Eves,' he announced. Herman, a fierce but kind man, had served the school well for years in many capacities. He was to die soon after he retired. Somervell, a remarkable man, with more talent than most of his colleagues, was liberal and tolerant – a gifted historian and teacher of English. Judde House, in his time, had the reputation for being good at music and not much else, and when they, to everyone's amazement, defeated Ferox Hall, with Cowdrey and several other 1st XI colours, Somervell – 'Slimey' as we called him – surprised everyone in the house, not only by watching, but also by struggling up from the town, carrying a crate of beer on his bicycle, which we drank in the showers. That night when I went to collect him for house prayers, he said 'What time does the party start?' and someone, contrary to the school rules, had to scoot down town on his bicycle to buy another crate.

In 1951 Ferdie Eames, Head of the Science Department, and ex-housemaster of Hill Side, retired. He also ran the school shop, and when Waddy said that he wanted all boys to carry their books in bags rather than in their arms, Ferdie devised a cheap leather and canvas bag which became known to generations as a 'Ferdie'. The term 'Ferdie' survived long after the man, who deserved a better epitaph. Ferdie was also the prime mover in the introduction of the new uniform – lovat suits and jackets, which were available only in his school shop. The lovat material was utilitarian, prickly and not very popular, but was meant to save parents money.

In Waddy's second year the number of Oxbridge scholarships rose to eight, and from then on academic standards began to rise steadily. By 1952 the school was bursting at the seams and it was necessary to open a waiting house, called Knox House, to take the overflow of boarders. Waddy forecast that Knox House was a temporary measure which would only last for four years. In fact it lasted 22 years and was one of the least satisfactory post-war innovations.

In 1952, also, the fiftieth anniversary of the chapel was celebrated by a thanksgiving service taken by the Archbishop of Canterbury, and *The Tonbridgian* issued a special Chapel Jubilee edition. Waddy announced plans to launch the Fourth Centenary Fund Appeal for 1953. T. Nottidge, a member of one of the school's oldest and most loyal families, retired after 27 years as secretary of the OT Society and George VI died, each marking the end of another era.

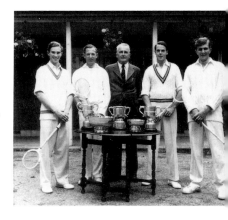

The school and OT rackets pairs of 1956–7 winners of the Public Schools Doubles and Singles, Amateur Doubles and Singles, and the Noel Bruce (Old Boys).

The Central Porch, 1953. This is one of a series of pictures drawn for the Quatercentenary Booklet in 1952 by Hervey Adams, the Art master.

The Queen Mother, seen with the Revd. L. H. Waddy and the Head Boy, R. E. Curnock, opened the Queen Mother's Gateway in 1953.

Frederick Forsyth, the novelist, was at the school from 1952–55.

1953 was to be a special year for the school as well as the country. Not only was it quatercentenary year and Coronation year, but the Coronation Lord Mayor of London was, by lucky chance, an OT – Sir Rupert de la Bère. Unfortunately another famous OT died that year – C. S. Kortright. Apart from being regarded by many as the fastest bowler ever, he had once conceded a 6 in byes!

The quatercentenary celebrations began with a visit by the Lord Mayor and an exhibition of school history. Welldon's punishment book of 100 years before was on display. Photos were taken of the school and of visiting OTs; cricket matches, meals and band concerts were laid on and the celebrations lasted three days, culminating in a service of commemoration conducted by the Bishops of Winchester and Edinburgh. Meanwhile it was announced that the Appeal had raised £10,000 for bursaries and £4,000 to build a fourth-centenary wall in front of the school to replace the railings removed during the War. So near the Coronation, there was no chance of the Queen visiting the school, but in October 1953, the Queen Mother came, named the new gateway with a boar's head mounted on each pillar as the Queen Mother's Gateway and charmed everyone, the boys in particular, by asking for them to be awarded an extra week's holiday.

The next ten years were a strange mixture of success and missed opportunity. Perhaps Waddy, with all his charm and versatility, was not exactly the leader the school needed. Perhaps he had less support from the housemasters than he might have expected: they felt there was not enough to support. Headmastering is a lonely job, and he lacked real friends. It did not help that the Chaplain was a housemaster and did not see eye to eye with him in either role. Waddy really believed in seeing the best of people and assumed everything was fine, whereas staff and boys alike respond better to a firmer rein. The Governors did not help by exercising such tight financial control that the school was beginning to look tatty.

Waddy was also housemaster of School House and was unfortunate in having some difficult boys there. With three young daughters and a wife who was beginning to suffer from severe and worrying ill-health, his problems must have sometimes seemed insurmountable, but he never dropped his air of cheery optimism. It is clear that few masters and even fewer boys knew the extent of the personal problems which were to remain with him until he left.

There were several good play productions, including two of Waddy's own. There was even a staff play, approximately 60 years after *The Tonbridgian* first requested one. The number of Oxbridge awards rose to a much more respectable level. School societies proliferated, and the abolition of National Service led to a major restructuring of the Corps and the introduction of the School Service Organization and the first arduous training expeditions to the Welsh mountains. Entrance applications continued to rise – a sure sign that all was reasonably well, and from about 1960 onwards, the 1st XI started on an immensely long period – almost 30 years – during which they lost hardly a school match, and the rackets players, boys and OTs, particularly Thompson, Gracey, Smith and Cowdrey, started to win so many rackets cups, including the Noel Bruce four years in succession, that they had to build a special case for them. Rylands and Connell won the Public Schools' rackets at Queen's, Tonbridge's first victory after 60 years of trying. Cowdrey and Marques played for England countless times. G. A. Hill captained the Walker Cup side and John Vigurs, who had never got into a school crew, rowed in the Olympics.

Changes were probably coming faster than people realized at the time, and several of the older members of staff retired over an eight-year period – Bathurst, Staveley, Hoole, Thomas, Morris, Reiss, Gray and McNeill, whose combined service totalled over 200 years, and whose dedication was immeasurable. Tragically, Peter Weaver died at an early age, just after taking over Welldon House, and Cecil Bullock died just before he was due to retire.

Sad as these losses were, the gaps created enabled Waddy to fill the school with new men, and he was either remarkably lucky or, more likely, remarkably astute in doing so. One of the strengths of Tonbridge over the last 30 years was the arrival during the 1950s and early 1960s of a very large group of young masters, some of whom have moved on to headmasterships elsewhere, but many of whom have stayed. Between them they offered a wide range of skills and interests, but mainly they liked each other and above all they liked the school.

The appointment of such excellent staff was Lawrence Waddy's greatest achievement. Modern generations will know the masters I mean and what they have done – several of them are still at the school. No OT can question their devotion or their range of talent. It is invidious to choose names from among them. Their arrival created the base on which many of Waddy's ideas could flourish, even though he himself decided to leave while these masters were still young. By 1962 he had been at the school 13 years; he had introduced several changes and he had probably shot his bolt. Many of his old boys regard him with great affection. 'I thought he was absolutely marvellous' – is a common reaction. Others say he did not give the lead the school needed. He was granted a sabbatical to teach at an American university, and James McNeill postponed his own retirement for a term to act as Headmaster, a job for which he was so well suited it made one realize how lucky Tonbridge had been to keep him for so long. While in America, Lawrence Waddy resigned and returned for only two more terms.

With his fresh outlook, Lawrence Waddy had laid the foundations, though no more, for guiding the school away from its pre-war ethos. Now the Governors had to consider where the school was to go in the 1960s, though they could not have foreseen what that particular decade had in store.

David Marques won 23 England caps.

Colin Cowdrey tossing up with Richie Benaud. Colin Cowdrey, a former Master of the Skinners' Company, is President of the OT Society. There are 7,000 OTs, of whom about 5,800 are members of the OT Society.

13

MICHAEL McCRUM

Never have there been so many changes in so short a time.

The Tonbridgian: *Editorial, 1967*

Michael McCrum, by Edmund Nelson.

When Lawrence Waddy announced his retirement, the Governors did not take long to choose his successor. The man they wanted was Michael McCrum, Tutor of Corpus Christi College. For some time the Skinners' Company, because of its origins as the Fraternity of the Body of Christ, had had links with Corpus Christi. McCrum was well known to the Skinners, and they saw in him the firm leader the school needed.

Michael McCrum, aged 38, educated at Sherborne and a classical scholar of Corpus, had spent two years as a master at Rugby, before returning to Cambridge for 12 years. He later married Christine, daughter of the Headmaster of Rugby. In persuading Michael McCrum to move from Cambridge, the Governors made what may be regarded as their most astute appointment yet.

McCrum arrived in September, and the Common Room welcomed him with immense goodwill and expectation, even though he had the advance reputation of being dictatorial. From the start he had total support from the Common Room and especially the housemasters, and he said recently, in an interview, that the Tonbridge housemasters at that time included some of the best he had ever come across. The housemasters, however, were not pleased by McCrum's totally unexpected suggestion that he would like to govern through a council of masters, on which each master would serve in turn for two years out of six. This was a dilution of their powers which they had not anticipated. McCrum maintained that he wanted to rule democratically. One housemaster, Dick Bradley, shortly to be made a headmaster himself, wrote to McCrum, pointing out that the Headmaster was the king, the housemasters the barons and the boys the peasants, and that he, McCrum, was paid to be king. So that is what McCrum reluctantly became. There were of course the cynics who claimed it was all a ploy on his part, but he maintains that he really did want to be a democrat. Once this problem had been ironed out, the masters settled

100

down to support him in everything he did. He proceeded to introduce democracy by another method, however, establishing committees on every aspect of school life. There was nothing new about this idea, but it was new to Tonbridge. Housemasters and Heads of Departments and several other committees now met regularly under his chairmanship, with proper minutes kept and distributed, and few masters did not find themselves on some committee or other.

On the other hand the boys regarded many of McCrum's early actions with suspicion and hostility. Lawrence Waddy had always appeared friendly and cheerful and would, one feels, rather have been one of the boys. Even when he had been at the school 13 years, Waddy still appeared extraordinarily young. Michael McCrum had a totally different appearance. He always wore a suit and looked older than his years. He was tall and dark and his gown seemed to go on for ever. He usually looked severe and did not smile too often, except when he was in his social mood. Boys found him, if not cold, then awesome, and the boys of the 1960s, embryonic flower-people, certainly did not see him as a flower-person. 'I was in awe of him,' is a comment OTs still make, as do more than a few masters.

The first edition of *The Tonbridgian* after his arrival reserved judgement, but at the end of his first term, three new editors were appointed who adopted a surprisingly hostile attitude towards him. Hidden in the 'School Notes' which followed the editorial, was a veiled attack on the new Headmaster, and the following issue contained a totally unjust attack on the Common Room for not working hard enough. It does show that there were boys at the top of the school who were not going to be easy to handle. McCrum himself, in his first Skinners' Day speech to parents, said that there was a general air of *malaise* in the school, but headmasters all over England were probably saying the same thing at that time.

McCrum was more sensitive to criticism than anyone realized, but he firmly believed that it was not a headmaster's duty to be popular, and he had a clear set of objectives which he carried out, regardless of the editors mentioned above. He had not, incidentally, received any briefing from the Governors, who merely watched and no doubt approved from afar.

What he achieved in eight years is so remarkable that the lasting benefits of his reign far outweigh any temporary difficulties it caused. He rarely stopped working, though he found time to tour the games fields almost every afternoon. He had been a good rugger player himself at school and university and was not above telling the XV that they could do better. He knew every boy and what he could achieve, usually well above what the boy himself contemplated; he and his wife knew every master and every member of his family. Christine was always the first on the doorstep in moments of crisis, offering to take someone to hospital or mind the children, though medical problems were most likely to involve the master himself – suffering from overwork. Between them they never stopped entertaining. One lost count of the number of lunch and dinner invitations, and an added bonus was that with their combined contacts, the other guests might well include a famous lecturer or politician. I shall never forget one famous woman journalist coming to lecture the VIth form on poverty, being entertained to the most sumptuous lunch afterwards, or on another occasion the doctor, who came to lecture the boys on the evils of smoking, destroying McCrum's hope that pipe-smoking did not count.

It was due to the McCrums' initiative that the Skinners' Library, formerly the Headmaster's dining-room – was converted to a luxurious drawing-room. Large French windows leading into the garden were built into the south wall, and this room, in which prospective parents are still interviewed, added considerably to the tone of the school.

It must be remembered that McCrum was severely handicapped by shortage of money. At one time things were so bad that, when it was suggested at a Common Room meeting that the porter's lodge should be manned throughout the day, McCrum said 'You can either have another porter or another master – you can't have both.' Waddy had had a blind spot over salaries, because he had absolutely no interest in money himself, and McCrum pleased the staff by raising their salaries considerably. Apart from that however, nearly all his innovations were non-financial, and they started to hit us almost from the first day. They ran almost parallel to the complaints in *The Tonbridgian*. The extraordinary thing is that McCrum introduced changes almost as fast as the staff could cope with them, and *The Tonbridgian* was crying out for changes, but not the ones he proposed. A letter from an OT at Oxford summed up the boys' feelings.

There are not enough outlets for self-expression.
There is too much conformity and interference with individual liberty.
There is insufficient challenge and stimulus to do anything worth while in the school.

These criticisms were probably all fair, for the petty rules and restrictions of the 1940s and 1950s still persisted. But McCrum tackled them in his own way, and if he did not succeed in removing them all in his time at Tonbridge, he created the basis on which his successors could do so, which is why it is essential to see his reign as part of the progressive development mentioned in Chapter 12.

The first thing he did was to change the curriculum and timetable. Three extra periods a week were added and the first-year curriculum adjusted, so that all novi coming into the school studied Science. He also introduced the unheard-of idea of all novi giving up French and Latin for their first few terms and doing Greek and German, Spanish or Russian instead. It was an imaginative idea, but it did not really work; it confused the boys and parents and worried prep school headmasters, though the scheme, in an adapted form, survived for many years. In the VIth form the extra periods were used for general studies.

After one year the school was subjected to an inspection. The inspectors' report was good as far as teaching was concerned, though it must be admitted that inspectors are not infallible. One master, who has now passed on, kept one brilliant lesson specially for them and reverted to type after they had left. In McCrum's second year the school obtained 13 Oxbridge awards, the highest total for some years. No doubt Lawrence Waddy took silent satisfaction as he read the results.

McCrum changed the pattern of chapel services so that boys no longer had to attend two services on Sunday, and together, he and the Chaplain, Harry Gripper, gave the weekday services more variety. He introduced prizes for initiative on Expedition Day so that boys got as far as Genoa and Edinburgh and back in one day. He greatly increased the number and value of entrance scholarships, and steadily improved the Common Entrance standard. He started parents' evenings for the first, third and final years – another move the boys did not like, as they never knew what masters were saying to their parents, and they felt the old days of playing the one off against the other had gone for good.

Normal school life proceeded as usual, except that everybody seemed to be working harder. C. H. Knott, always known as John, chose this moment to retire. He was a shy, silent man with an intensely devoted following of games-playing OTs. As a house tutor and housemaster for 35 years, he had suited some boys but not others. David Tomlinson, the actor, is outspoken about him in his autobiography, but few of the boys realized what stature John had had in his younger days as a Kent cricketer, and he was highly thought of outside the school. If I may reminisce: in my first year on the staff I gave out his best batsman lbw on the front foot in a house match. He let me know, via a colleague, that lbw on the front foot was an abominable modern idea. On his retirement he took over the school register, so that he was able to complete 70 years of his life at Tonbridge, watching the cricket on the Head till just before he died. Arthur Hull retired after 50 years as rackets professional in a year when the school pair reached the final at Queen's, and Eric Payne after 50 years, most of them as senior lab. assistant. It is a sad reflection on life at Tonbridge that Hull was given a farewell dinner at the Rose and Crown, while Payne only got a clock! Both gentlemen were interviewed on 'Down Your Way' when it came to the town and spoke sincerely of their devotion to the school.

McCrum's first term had witnessed the opening of the new South Wing, the money for which had been raised by appeal. It contained the new Smythe Library, the new house tutor's house for School House and the cloister running the length of the building, named Ironside cloister. In November Princess Alexandra opened the building, looking charming in spite of the rain, particularly so as she was to announce her engagement two days later. She endeared herself to the boys by sitting next to them at tea and insisting on visiting those parts of the School House which the authorities had decided to steer her away from. The new South Wing was mainly Waddy's brainchild, and it was greeted with mixed feelings. It was a gallant attempt by Lord Holford to blend a modern building with an old one, combating a slope in the process, but as a library, meant to double as a work place for VIth formers, it soon turned out to be too small. It is beautiful inside, but externally it is open to criticism, especially on account

Edmund Ironside is Tonbridge's most famous soldier. He is probably best known for his command of the British Expedition to Russia at the end of the Great War. He was CIGS in 1940. The cloister leading to the school library, where this plaque and other plaques are installed, is called the Ironside cloister.

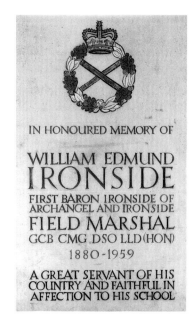

of its windows. Rain from the lead in the surrounds started to stain the stone as soon as they were put in. Princess Alexandra, while shaking Lord Holford's hand, looked round at the building and said with a smile, 'If it rains much longer, it'll turn brown!'

In his first Skinners' Day speeches to parents McCrum set out his objectives and defended the position of public schools. His speeches make better reading than listening, and I wish there were space to quote them as they give a good insight into the depth and breadth of his vision, though they are not overflowing with humour.

Quick to seize on any new idea going, McCrum readily accepted Alfred Foster's wish to install a Language Laboratory, and the one which was opened in 1963 was one of the first in the country. Other changes soon followed: a new prospectus and a new school list with the masters now listed in alphabetical order, causing those in the bottom half of the alphabet to complain bitterly that they had struggled for years to get on to the first page, and now found themselves relegated to the second page again; boxing was banned on medical grounds and replaced by judo; driving lessons were introduced; and the next Head of School's appointment was deferred for a term as a punishment for bowling underarm in a school match as a protest against being no-balled.

A new organization was set up for novi – the Terriers – now that government regulations no longer allowed them to join the Corps until they were older, and the Mitchell Cup, the house cup for Corps efficiency, drilled and sweated for by so many for so long, was abolished. McCrum, an ex-naval officer, had a dislike for drill, regarding it as a waste of time, just as he disliked the school songs, which he thought gave the school an outmoded Victorian image. A German television company spent a great deal of time and money filming the school. The film was shown in Germany at peak viewing time, but we thought it completely failed to capture the feel of the school, though changes were happening so fast, even we did not know where we were. At the same time a group of boys under Dick Bradley produced *Tonbridge*, a short book which gave a much more accurate view of the school as it was in 1965.

On Skinners' Days McCrum was able to report on some striking achievements during this time. Monteuuis won the rackets singles at Queen's, four OTs contested the Amateur Doubles rackets finals, and the 1st XI hardly lost a school match during this decade. On one occasion the Lords match took place before the end of term and the whole school was bussed to Lords, an experiment never to be repeated, thank goodness. Coloured immigration was only just starting, and the boys on my house bus hurled their pork pies at the new arrivals as they passed through Brixton. They would not dare do it today. The Lords match was soon to be reduced to a one-day match and in 1969 to disappear altogether to be replaced by the Eastbourne Festival.

In 1965 D. C. Somervell died. Owen Chadwick, soon to be elected Regius Professor of Modern History at Cambridge, wrote a marvellous obituary of him in *The Tonbridgian*. Here is a brief extract: 'Somervell was unquestionably a great teacher. It is hard to say why. He conformed to none of the rules, passed few of the ordinary tests. . . . His lectures were perfectly arranged. It was impossible to misunderstand his meaning. It was impossible for him to be dull.' McCrum once said that Somervell's *History of Tonbridge School* was the best school history ever written. It was short, humorous and written, apparently, straight out of his head over the period of a few weeks. Ah well!

At the end of 1965 McCrum abolished fagging. He had already stopped boys beating other boys and made beating by housemasters a rare event; he had virtually dismantled the privilege system and now – at one fell swoop – he took an axe to the long-established hierarchical structure of the school. There were agonized protests from many quarters, especially those who had been fags in their youth and were looking forward to reaping the reward. It was feared that this reduction in praes' privileges would reduce their authority. This latter criticism was probably true, and praes have definitely had a harder job since. Nevertheless, one of McCrum's greatest assets was his ability to see ahead, and he knew the time had come to end what he saw as an anachronism.

He introduced the 'Senior Student' system, whereby boys in their last term or two could apply to leave their boarding-houses and go and live in a Senior Student house to have some privacy and work in an atmosphere more resembling that of a university staircase. Over the years this system has benefited hundreds of boys. Though the boys continued to eat and play games with their senior house, some housemasters did not like the system. Some have used it to be shot of their troublemakers, some to move their heads of house upstairs after a term or two to give the promotion ladder a boost. The result was frequently a strange mix of senior boys thrown together at the end of their careers in the care of a new housemaster. It provided good training for living on a university staircase.

I was given the care of the first Senior Student house. One of my innovations was to allow boys to entertain girls in their rooms in the afternoon. For Tonbridge this was quite a departure. One afternoon, soon after the house opened, a pretty but rather scatty girl was visiting the captain of rugger. He was out playing rugger. She suddenly heard the Headmaster's voice and hid in the wardrobe. McCrum was showing the new rooms to some Governors. She heard him go into the room next door and open the fitted wardrobe: 'As you see,' he said, 'the boys have everything provided!' Then they went downstairs.

In future scholars would take two years to reach O level instead of one, to prevent their passing through the school too quickly, and, at the top end, an élite Upper VIth was created. New Maths was introduced, and a new psalter in chapel. House debating contests were established and became very popular, and a naval section was formed. From now on boys were allowed to visit the town cinema and a coffee bar in the High Street, and praes could go to pubs for meals. The rules about boys visiting boys in other houses were relaxed, and boys were allowed to wear casual clothes in their houses in the evenings. Twenty-five years on these relaxations of the rules may seem trivial, but at the time they were not, and they formed an essential part of McCrum's strategy. Even *The Tonbridgian* wrote in 1967: 'Never have there been so many changes in so short a time.' Their pace was too fast for some of the boys and not fast enough for others.

Tonbridge for many years was unusual in that every year a statement of the school's income and expenditure account was published in the OT Letter, including the net income from the Foundation and the total of masters' salaries. In the 1966 Letter there was a letter from McCrum referring to the school's financial position, and the accounts were prefaced by a statement repeating what McCrum had said in his letter, that is, that the school was heavily in the red to the tune of £120,000. Economies must be made; the endowment had been eroded by inflation; no increased income could be expected from the Foundation for many years because the school property was let on long leases, and the deficit must be reduced.

Part of the deficit was cleared by selling two of the school playing-fields near the sanatorium, on which the purchasers built a large private housing estate. The price they obtained for this land now seems low, but when is the right moment, if ever, to sell land? Under McCrum's skilful management the large deficit was wiped out within a few years, though working under financial restraints could not have made his job easier.

The changes continued apace. Form III was abolished, meaning that the Common Entrance standard was raised still further; a system of senior tutors was introduced for VIth-formers. Novi visits were started: in future all candidates for Common Entrance were invited to spend a day and night at the school at the end of the preceding Lent term. The 'Novi Visit' has been a regular feature of school life since then. It has had several consequences, not all of them intentional. It has enabled boys, housemasters and parents to have a good look at each other in advance, so that when the boy does join the school, homesickness lasts a few hours rather than a few days; some boys have been accepted who might otherwise have been rejected, and you can now be certain that the weather during those two days will be awful. Any boy who can climb a rope, crawl through a pipe, do an IQ test, run a hundred yards and read a poem aloud, frozen to the marrow and breathless to exhaustion, must know that things after he joins the school can only get better. Anyway, most of them go home determined to pass Common Entrance, and only one to my knowledge has withdrawn as a consequence.

Compulsory Corps was abolished in 1968 and a variety of alternative activities arranged for which boys could opt instead of joining the Corps. A system of house 'circuses' was introduced in the winter term – a kind of league or round-robin competition, covering a variety of sports not normally played. A climbing-wall was built for the Climbing Club, and for the masters an annual Common Room dinner was introduced.

Hervey Adams retired in 1963 and Allan Bunney in 1967. Few schools could have had such a gifted pair in charge of their Art and Music

'The Skinners' Library', by F. P. Barraud, 1891. F. P. Barraud specialized in painting school scenes. His picture of the Skinners' Library shows the room as it was in Victorian times. The original is hanging in the Skinners' Library. The portrait of Vicesimus Knox II seen over the fireplace has unfortunately since disappeared.

recent picture of cricket on the Head on a mid-week afternoon.

departments. Hervey's last year was marked by an exhibition of the work of some of his Old Boys, including Wishaw, Higgins and Thomas. Allan Bunney's last year was celebrated by the BBC choosing to record 'Songs of Praise' from the school chapel. Several letters were received, mostly of appreciation, but one listener did write, 'If these boys can do top E flat, surely with a lozenge of some kind they can squeeze E without creaking, croaking or choking.' Dr Bunney was replaced by John Cullen, and soon class teaching in music was introduced for the whole school and one musical firebrand was replaced by another.

In 1968 McCrum announced the setting up of the XXth Century Fund Appeal to provide continuous finance for a string of projects, the most important of which was the development of the Potkiln Farm area for the building of a running-track and hard hockey-pitch with further pitches alongside. It was the first major development for some time, and it was hoped that a new theatre would be built before long. This was particularly important as the number and quality of dramatic productions, especially house plays, was rising fast. The annual Shakespeare productions had been replaced by more modern plays, and Jonathan Smith's productions of *Rosencrantz and Guildenstern are Dead* and *Royal Hunt of the Sun* had both stunned the audience and made the lack of a proper theatre more evident.

In 1968 Stan Twort retired after 31 years as head groundsman and in his last year had the pleasure of seeing some of his favourite Old Boys distinguish themselves. Colin Cowdrey chose Skinners' Day and a Test match against Australia to score his hundredth first-class century, and in the same series Roger Prideaux made his Test début. David Toft and David Aers were on opposite sides in the Varsity match at Lords. Meanwhile the Welldon House junior side were all out for nought in a house match, nine runs less than their senior house team scored in their match. McCrum was a strong supporter of school sport, but he did not allow many additions to the fixture list, mainly for financial reasons. He did not approve of golf or bridge, regarding them as time-wasting.

In the winter term 1969 Michael McCrum and Christine threw a wild party at which he announced that he had accepted the headmastership of Eton – the first Headmaster to go to Eton for 300 years. Many of the staff were disappointed by the news, and he had tears in his eyes when he made the announcement because he genuinely enjoyed Tonbridge.

Before he left he introduced a few more changes. He persuaded the housemasters to accept the idea of elected praes, but he failed to persuade the Common Room to accept the idea of a School Council. In July 1970 the Common Room put on a farewell supper followed by a revue, which pilloried him unmercifully. In his party mood he took it on the chin with a smile, and Christine cried with laughter. General opinion was that he had done a marvellous job. Perhaps OTs who read this chapter will see why. In eight years he had taken the school apart and put it back twice. When he left, he was beginning to show alarming signs of wanting to do it again.

King Lear. *Jeffery Summers, unlike Hoffy Arnold, believed in scenery. John Bowis is now one of six OT members of Parliament. Nick Hornsby won three rowing blues for Cambridge.*

14

ROBERT OGILVIE

What boys say is something one must pay an enormous amount of attention to. They're the consumers and if they are not getting the right thing, then it is very important that they should.

Dr R. M. Ogilvie, 1971

Robert Ogilvie, by Derek Hill.

Can you imagine any of the previous 27 Headmasters saying that in an interview? Can you imagine Cawthorn saying it? The new Headmaster did, and nobody seemed to mind, because he was such an affable man.

After eight years of McCrum the school needed a breather, and the Governors knew it. Again they went to a university for their new Headmaster, this time to Oxford, and invited another senior tutor to undertake the challenge of headmastering. Robert Ogilvie was Senior Tutor of Balliol. He had been educated at Rugby and won a scholarship to Balliol, where he had won honour after honour in classics. His parents had both been principals of Oxford Colleges, his father of Jesus and his mother of St Anne's. He himself had been at Oxford for 20 years and felt that he needed a new challenge, and he seemed to be just the sort of man Tonbridge needed to build on McCrum's changes and give them a human touch. Before he came, he decided he did not wish to be a housemaster, and J. K. Ind was appointed to be housemaster of School House.

Soon after he arrived in 1970, Ogilvie gave an interview to *The Tonbridgian* which revealed his thinking on education. There is not room to print the whole interview, but a summary says much about the man.

His main interests were classics and music. He was particularly interested in the effect of classics on English life and education. He himself played the piano and the cello. He was a passionate Scot, so much so that he seemed to lead a double life. On the one hand he had been educated and made his living in England, on the other he had a house in Scotland to which he and his family fled as often as possible. His love of Scotland and climbing combined well with his passion for Scottish history and archaeology. One of his brothers had been killed climbing the Matterhorn with a brilliant OT, J. I. C. McKean.

He believed that education meant trying to create the means of maximizing people's abilities within the happiest possible framework. In a public school or university setting, this meant developing the individual while teaching him to live together with others. He believed that scientists should be more literate and arts men more numerate. He did not believe in trying to teach university subjects at school level. Those were his views in a nutshell, and they sound rather ordinary, but he turned out to be a far from ordinary Headmaster. His mind ranged over a whole variety of subjects, and he read at great speed.

He had a very different personality from his predecessor, and on his arrival he met with a mixed reception. The housemasters were initially baffled by him. They were possibly overawed by his academic pedigree, while he was painfully aware that they knew much more about schoolmastering than he did. Relations were tentative. He was even more baffled to find that much of his first housemasters' meeting was devoted to the thorny question of clothing and that he was expected to decide whether the current desire of boys to wear Chelsea boots should be approved or not. To his annoyance, no doubt, much of his time was to be spent arguing about the width of trouser-legs, the length of hair, at what hours jeans were permissible and where they could be worn. He did not find administration difficult; he was capable of rising early and clearing his desk before breakfast, and he had the kind of mind which could embrace any problem and find an immediate solution, but he must have found the minutiae of administration tedious. He continued to chair all the committees which McCrum had started, but he did not seem to enjoy them and took refuge in his endless supply of cigars. Likewise he did not enjoy HMC conferences and committees and, unlike McCrum, did not play much of a role at HMC.

The boys, on the other hand, took to him almost immediately and were soon laughing at his obvious failings. He was prone to exaggeration and he was a great name-dropper. In spite of his intellect, he was able to communicate with boys better than with masters. Obviously he enjoyed the company of clever boys, but he also had a sneaking affection for the miscreant. He felt that the best thing to do with a boy with problems was take him off and play golf with him and give him a cheese sandwich. Even though he was not housemaster of School House, he was always dropping in on the boys there.

To a schoolboy populace, few of whom ever travelled north of London, he wove an air of mystery round his Scottish background. Even if he did not own vast Scottish estates as he sometimes hinted, he claimed kinship with most of those who did. The boys said that he employed tricks on the golf-course of a devious Scottish nature, which is interesting because both his predecessors also hated losing at games.

Once a trivial dispute with a few senior boys was settled, his relations with the boys remained excellent, and to some extent he was able to carry out the ideas expressed at the beginning of this chapter. By the time

Ogilvie left, the boys at least felt that what they thought mattered: McCrum's many changes had become part of everyday routine; Ogilvie introduced a few more of his own and the combined effect of the two reigns was a much more modern school and a much better one than McCrum had taken over.

The early 1970s turned out to be a period of rising inflation, and Ogilvie was clearly alarmed at the prospect of hyper-inflation. Although the school was full and the high number of Oxbridge awards each year ensured full entrance lists, he had a natural caution about spending money, and most of the changes he made did not involve finance, though some of the more important problems facing the school might have done. There was a very large increase in the number of day-boy applicants and the two day-boy houses were bursting at the seams. Should a third day-boy house be built? Boarding numbers were remaining static, as the houses were full, but four of the boarding-houses to the north of the London Road, as well as the 1st- and 2nd-XV grounds, were threatened by a new inner bypass. Would it be better therefore to plan for the future and build new houses within the perimeter? Should the school follow the modern trend and admit girls at VIth form level? Should housemasters' wives be relieved of the constant worry of finding catering staff by going over to central feeding?

These problems consumed much time at housemasters' meetings and, no doubt, much of Ogilvie's attention. In the end it was decided to open a new day-boy house but Ogilvie was firmly against the admission of girls (his mother was a governor of three girls' schools) and against central feeding, which some housemasters or their wives badly wanted. An outside catering firm was engaged, with a resident catering manager, so that Tonbridge is one of the few schools with all its houses still eating in their dining-rooms.

Ogilvie was able to share the school's enjoyment of McCrum's last great scheme – the levelling of the old Potkiln Farm area and the installation of a running-track and all-weather hockey-pitch, which were opened in 1971, at the same time as the new Tonbridge outer bypass, which reduced the traffic passing by the school. Life for the boys was getting easier too, and *The Tonbridgian*, contrary as ever, complained that less discipline is not necessarily a good thing.

A VIth-form centre opened where senior boys could relax, entertain girls and hold intelligent conversations; exeats were made longer, and a long postal strike enabled boys to abandon for ever the art of letter-writing and demand the installation of more phones in boarding-houses.

In the 1970s the 1st XI started another purple patch, the OTs kept winning the Noel Bruce rackets cup, and also reached the Cricketer Cup final four years in succession, winning it in 1971 and 1972. The first victory against Charterhouse was decided on a faster scoring rate after the umpires had decided no further play was possible, which led to another Charterhouse objection; you may remember that they objected to Tonbridge winning in 1903. The Cricketer Cup was sponsored by the Moët et Chandon champagne company and the cup was presented by their

David Walsh, John Knott, and Mike Bushby, between them ran the cricket for over 60 years up until 1986.

vice-president, who clearly did not understand English or cricket, let alone run rates, which were worked out by E. W. Swanton with a calculator.

In 1972 two old school institutions disappeared. The House singing competition – the 'House Shout' – was replaced by a school performance of 'Carmina Burana' and George Cooper, the bandmaster retired. Like the school songs and the Gilbert and Sullivan, the House Shout has never been satisfactorily replaced, and the present non-marching band is a poor substitute for George Cooper's old one, with its tattoos and processions and invitations to play at the Royal Tournament. In the course of all the changes which happened in the 1960s and 1970s, some things like the House Shout, the Gilbert and Sullivan, the Sing Songs and the marching band, were thrown away, which with hindsight might have been preserved.

Winning Cricketer Cup team at Gatwick, 1971. For many years the Cricketer Cup was sponsored by Moët et Chandon. The prize, apart from lavish supplies of champagne, was a week-end for the winning team at the Moët et Chandon château at Epernay. After Tonbridge had won the cup two years running, the prize was changed to a day's outing with wives and girl friends invited too, to add a touch of restraint.

Soon after Ogilvie's arrival three of the most respected ex-masters died within eight weeks of one another: Whitworth, Vere Hodge and Eames; and in 1971, three senior masters retired, all of them housemasters in their time: Foster, Lake and Hedley-Jones. Ted Whenday, school porter since time immemorial, also retired, and soon there would be few pre-war faces left. A year later Jack Clifton retired from the school shop after many years behind the counter. Better known to OTs than any other person at Tonbridge, his extraordinary memory and fund of anecdotes deserve a book of their own.

In 1971 Ogilvie reinstituted the post of Second Master, defunct since the death of E. I. Welldon nearly a hundred years earlier. After Welldon's death the senior assistant master was paid an extra £5 per anum: this sum was still being paid in 1960. As Second Master Ogilvie appointed David Kemp, housemaster of Park House and an OT, one of those dedicated schoolmasters who exist in every school, never seek the limelight and receive their reward in heaven. Ogilvie himself was elected a Fellow of the British Academy, a very rare distinction for a schoolmaster.

Ogilvie set about introducing some innovations of his own. Reunions by decades were organized by Vernon Hedley-Jones, so that every year about 250 OTs return to see how the school has advanced or gone to the dogs. This event does the school more good than any other event, and the goodwill it generates far outweighs any expenditure on it. One Old Boy, returning home by train after attending a reunion, was sitting next to a man of his own age and told him where he had been. 'You are lucky', said the man who had been to a maintained secondary school, 'to have roots to go back to!'

Many minor structural improvements were started, but money now had to come from the XXth Century Appeal Fund. Once some of the lesser

OGLETHORPE?.... WHY YES,
HE WAS HERE A COUPLE OF
MINUTES AGO

Annual OT reunions by age-groups were started in 1972. Average attendance is about 250. When H. D. Mallet, a famous cartoonist and contributor to Punch *attended the 1987 reunion, he drew a set of cartoons of the occasion and presented them to the school. H. F. Ellis is another OT with connections with* Punch.

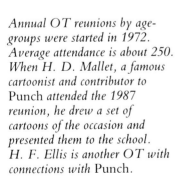

projects were completed, money was collected for the new indoor swimming-pool to be built at the far end of Martin's.

Ogilvie's educational philosophy can be summed up in four words: 'It should be fun!' and that is what it was under him. *The Tonbridgian* reflects it. There were myriad societies, countless school trips, theatre visits etc. and the staff and boys felt far more relaxed. Willy-nilly, the third stage in the school's post-war metamorphosis was happening.

Ogilvie continued to express pessimism about the future of private schools. In fact, the continual threats to public schools, the egalitarian ideas of the Schools Council, the attacks on competitiveness all helped schools like Tonbridge. The Governors changed their policy and numbers shot up from 572 in 1971 to 634 in 1975. Knox House, the waiting house, was converted into the third day-boy house: Whitworth House named after the great war-time Headmaster. The idea was to reduce the other two day-boy houses to 55 each, but within a few years all three were up to 70 or more. More Senior Student houses were opened, and in many ways the school buzzed.

The cricket XI, while flourishing, suffered from the death of Ray Dovey, the much-loved coach, and the retirement of Mike Bushby as master in charge, after 16 years of almost unbroken success. The rackets pair of Nigel Hawkins and Chris Cowdrey won the Public Schools doubles, and the XV continued to stretch everyone's nerves with a string of moral victories. The Corps was now in the hands of its first full-time commander, Lt.-Col. Russell, straight from the Army, and the Astronomical Society hit the headlines by having the only telescope in the country to observe that an expected great astronomical event did not happen: it was a very cloudy night and all the others could not see. How do you win a prize for a non-event? Professor Barton (OT), who had won a Nobel Prize for Chemistry, came and lectured and said that what he had learnt was mainly learnt after Tonbridge. In fact he left when he was still quite young.

It was a lively school under Ogilvie, but, after only five years, Robert Ogilvie resigned and accepted one of the three posts he always said he would like, the professorship of Humanity at St Andrew's University. The calls of classical scholarship and Scotland were too great for him. He always claimed to be an optimist, but, in fact, he was a pessimist, and perhaps he felt that he was not cut out to be a headmaster. He was, however, far more popular than he realized; the boys even gathered outside his house before breakfast to sing 'Happy Birthday', and, when he departed, there was widespread sadness. On the last day of his last term, on Skinners' Day, the Master of the Skinners' Company, Michael Marriott, opened the magnificent new swimming-pool. Many of us regretted the closing of the old open-air pool off the Hadlow Road. The trouble with working in a school is that too often you have to witness the end of institutions, which, to you, seem perfectly satisfactory, and see people leave whom you wish would stay.

HULLO-ULLO-ULLO, SIR... REMEMBER ME?....
SMITH, J?.. DAY BOYS B?..'30-'31?....er..

15

CHRISTOPHER EVERETT

I don't care so much about the music, but, boy, those accents!
Comment by one of the audience during the choir tour of the USA
1980

Christopher Everett, by
Daphne Todd, RP, NEAC.

The Governors appointed Christopher Everett, Headmaster of Worksop College, to succeed Robert Ogilvie. He was the first new Headmaster of Tonbridge since the War to have had experience as a headmaster, though, surprisingly, he had never been an assistant master. As a boy at Winchester, he won a classical exhibition to New College. Before going to Oxford he did his national service as an officer in the Guards and, after Oxford, joined the Diplomatic Service. He was sent to the Lebanon to learn Arabic and later served in London and in Washington.

After ten years as a diplomat, he decided he would like to be a headmaster and was appointed Headmaster of Worksop in 1970, where he quickly established a reputation of which the Governors were well aware. When he came to Tonbridge in September 1975, he was 42 years old, married with four children. Soon after he arrived he was shocked, like everyone else at Tonbridge, by the death of Michael Marriott (OT), Master of the Skinners' Company, who had for many years devoted so much of his spare time and energy to the school.

So we come to the last chapter of this long post-war section. The school had changed a great deal in the previous 26 years. Waddy, McCrum and Ogilvie, very different from one another, had each brought new ideas with which to tackle the problems of a rapidly changing world. The school was full for years ahead, but it was still not well known nationally. To be fair, it had never tried to be or wanted to be. It was content to do its best in the limited but desirable confines of Kent. Its reputation as a school with too much emphasis on sport had been replaced by a reputation for being too science-orientated and having too high a pass mark at Common Entrance. Also, it had been rather unfairly depicted in the film *If*.

Within a short time of his arrival, Everett transformed the school in two ways. First, with his own drive and personality, he gave the school a reputation which extended far beyond the South-East. He was the most impressive of figures whenever he stood up at a Headmasters' conference or a prep school prize-giving. He seemed to be able to talk, without notes and with great knowledge, on any educational subject. He impressed parents and prep school headmasters to a degree which no other Tonbridge Headmaster had done. He was always travelling and promoting the school without being pushy. He had the marvellous knack of turning up at any school event which mattered and making the boys feel he was interested: choir recitals in Paris, Corps camps, Cricketer Cup finals, to mention just a few.

The second way in which he really left his mark on Tonbridge was just a reflection of his own personality. He was not only the most optimistic man any of us had ever met, at least on the surface, he was also the most enthusiastic and energetic. It seemed as if his wife, Billie, wound him up every morning, pointed him in the direction of his study and sent him off.

It took a little time for the boys to get used to him, particularly as Robert Ogilvie was remembered with affection and loyalty by many of the senior boys; but very soon his ready wit and irrepressible good humour won them over. Soon after his arrival he was being photographed for *The Tonbridgian* in all kinds of unlikely poses. He was an easy man to make fun of, and he accepted the barbs with good grace: he was also very photogenic. He hardly ever sat down, and when he did, he contorted his long legs into the most extraordinary positions, which delighted the boys. He was at heart far too soft, and the boys knew it; discipline was not his strong point, nor that of his deputy, David Kemp, so that later they had to create a new post – that of Third Master – whose main task was to enforce discipline. As the first master to fill this post, Hugh Tebay, son of a policeman, was able to show his talent both as a law-and-order man and as a psychologist.

Christopher Everett was to stay 14 years – long enough to leave a deep impression on the school. He was an excellent administrator and committee chairman. He was at his best at masters' meetings, which he always conducted standing up. He astounded everyone with his memory, his grasp of all the changes taking place in the educational system, his knowledge of every boy, but above all with his repartee. Some of his retorts at masters' meetings were stunning without being hurtful. He was adept at soothing feelings and finding the humour in any situation. Everyone has faults, and his main one was procrastination. He shelved decisions with the Foreign Office attitude that everything would work out. 'Let's see how it goes!' was one of his favourite expressions.

Under him many things came right which had not seemed right before, as though he was tying up the loose ends left by his predecessors. Suddenly, most people seemed happy; not everyone because he did talk a great deal and sometimes seemed not to be listening. In fact he was listening because he often quoted back at you much later what you had said months or even years before. He overawed some parents by talking in

Dorothy Chard
Sanatorium Matron

Cecil Bullock
Assistant Master

Allan Walter Bunney
Director of Music

William Preston Lake
Housemaster

Dorothy Knott
Housekeeper

Nesta Dence
Music Staff

Remi Whenday
Works Staff

Theodore Dewey
Medical Officer

A page from the Book of Remembrance in the chapel The Book of Remembrance commemorates all those who have died who served the school for more than ten years. The pages are turned regularly.

The school choir on the steps of the Capitol, 1990. The choir, which these days contains trebles from Yardley Court, had been singing in Washington Cathedral.

educational terms they had never heard of. He had so many ideas and was full of so many plans that inevitably some of them did not mature. Never mind – he was right for Tonbridge and Tonbridge was right for him. Near the end of his time he almost became Headmaster of his old school, Winchester. When he was not chosen, he was clearly disappointed, but nearly everyone at Tonbridge, especially the boys, heaved a sigh of relief.

When I started to write this book, I set out with the idea of showing that Tonbridge's success, if that is what it is, was brought about by above-average results on the games field and a succession of good headmasters. My studies show that the sporting results have been good, but, with the exception of cricket and rackets, not outstanding.

The Headmasters, on the other hand, have nearly all been very good. Consultations with colleagues and Old Boys about the validity of this thesis have thrown up two other factors which should not be left out. The first is that the recent prosperity in the South-East has led to the influx into the area of a large number of 'attainers'. They are mainly accountants, brokers or entrepreneurs, but they are successful and very interested in their sons' education. They are intelligent and so are their sons. The academic standard has rocketed since the War, and this is particularly so of the day-boy population, which has provided some very bright boys indeed.

The other factor is the quality of the Common Room. For many years the Common Room has been happy and united and has contained several outstanding men, totally devoted to the school. Some have moved on to headmasterships elsewhere; but many others have stayed for their whole working lives. I would like to name at least a dozen or more, but I can't – it would be invidious to do so. Frankly, the boys have been lucky with their masters in recent years, even if they didn't realize it, and, on the whole, the masters have been lucky with the boys.

The amount of drama, music, foreign trips, adventure holidays and sport is staggering, as it no doubt is at all similar schools. The number of petty rules has been sharply reduced, though, in an institution which takes boys from 13 to 18, the latter may still feel restricted. The boys on the whole are cheerful, if rather untidy, and the housemasters work hours which would drive some people to an early grave.

Parents have more say in what goes on; the boys go home more often; the Old Tonbridgians maintain the right mix of interest and detachment; and the one thing which is really wrong is that the attractions of a well-paid future in the City or in advertising are too seductive. Obviously there have been several who have succeeded away from the City, like Owen Chadwick, Patrick Mayhew, John Leahy, Freddie Forsyth, Sandy Wilson and Tim Severin. Occasionally, at the Old Boys' reunion, one meets an OT who has become something really unusual, like Phil Sargisson, a United Nations' Commissioner for Refugees, but such examples are too few.

Everett's reign must wait for a proper assessment from the next historian, but of his time a few other events should be mentioned. The

Governors sold the Baths playing-fields and purchased the Hawden fields between the school and the river, so that the school now has over 60 more acres of fields within the perimeter. A new technology department, a school laundry and a new building for School House were all built in his time. Exchanges have been established with schools in France, Spain, Germany and Austria, and Russia may well follow. Drama has increased to the extent where the number of school and house productions far exceeds the facilities to stage them.

Under Everett the academic results continued to rise. He was a past master at making the A level results seem better every year, thereby enabling him most years to award the school an extra holiday. One year the results were not quite so good, by one-tenth of one per cent. He pointed out that if a certain boy called X (an OT's son) had left a year before as he suggested, this disaster would not have happened. In 1982, in the year before Oxbridge entrance scholarships were abolished, the boys won 17 open awards, not a record, but better than any other boarding school of Tonbridge's size, and by 1982 it was much harder to win awards than it had been ten years earlier. Much of the credit for these results must go to the Science, Maths and English departments, particularly the first, who still have to teach in the 1887 building, which is perfectly serviceable, though it could do with more small lecture rooms.

Music under John Cullen and drama under a variety of producers make good use of many boys' time. About 300 boys learn instruments, and the choir, the orchestra and the band are always going off to perform in America or Vienna or Paris, and Everett, in his time, was usually there to hear them. Drama he boosted in person by insisting on appearing in all staff plays, usually acting the part of a policeman and playing to the audience at the same time.

He took a firm decision to invest heavily in electronics. A new electronics building and head of department, computer room and computer network, now connecting all the boarding-houses, master-minded initially by Dick Longley, are examples of this. The school was one of the first to go in for computers, and Acorn Computers regard us as leaders in this area. They use pictures of Tonbridge in their latest adverts, so that when you are watching ITV, pictures of the front of the school suddenly flash in front of your eyes.

The boys entered the BP 'Build a Robot' competition, for which they had to design an electronic butler –'Garfield' – to serve drinks. They would have won, but Garfield, having served the drinks, disgraced himself in front of the Duke of Kent, by failing to return to his pantry, and they came second. Meanwhile the Head of Technical Activities, Tim Hughes, announced proudly that for the first time ever his department had outspent the rugger players and he now had his eyes on the cricketers. Tim Hughes happens to be one of the top radio hams in the country and keeps boys busy listening in, hoping to contact King Hussein. One afternoon one of them picked up a voice from the desert. 'I think I've got something, Sir,

The Tonbridge entry in the BP 'Build a Robot' competition reached the final four. The robot had to take an order, serve a drink and return to its base. Initially, 'Garfield' performed perfectly. It went into the pub, appropriately named the Boar's Head, served the drink, and then lost its bearings, which it had never done before. Ray Bradley, the master-in-charge of Computing, blamed the large number of photographers' flash-bulbs.

The school golf team of 1986 won the England and European Schools championships, a double achieved only once before – by our neighbours at the Hugh Christie School, Tonbridge. Team: D. Ellis, E. Richardson, D. Wood.

The School 1st and 2nd pairs of 1984–5, winners of the Public Schools Singles and Doubles in the Senior and Under-16 categories.

have a listen!' Tim went on the line. 'I recognize that voice,' said the other end, 'It's Mr Hughes, isn't it?' It wasn't King Hussein. It was an OT crossing the Sahara in a jeep.

Everett was a great supporter of games, though he never intended to put them on a pedestal. These years saw a string of successes, some of them areas where we had not done well before. In 1986 the school golf team won the Kent, England and European schools championships. In 1985 the OTs won the Glenfarcas Old Boys' Cup for hockey. Between 1981 and 1987 the school rackets players won the Public Schools doubles five times and the singles four times in succession. Much of the credit for this must go to David Makey, the young coach, and Dr Batterby, the master in charge, but the school was lucky to have an influx of very good games players at that time, many of them brothers like the Cowdreys, Ellisons, Spurlings, Owen-Brownes and Longleys.

Rackets is a strange obsession: you either love it or hate it. Those who hate it regard it as élitist and expensive. Everett loved it and attended the finals at Queen's without fail, just as he watched cricket as often as possible, even though he frequently stood there clapping and shouting 'good shot', when it wasn't. He was very keen on matches and gave his support to the introduction of block fixtures so that on some Saturdays over 20 teams – half the school – might be playing against Wellington or Dulwich. At the same time the fixture list has been revised and improved, so that the plaintive wish for better opponents expressed in that *Tonbridgian* letter of over 120 years ago has been granted.

The OTs won the Cricketer Cup three more times in Everett's early years and the players took him (and me) to Epernay to the Moët et Chandon château as a reward for faithful support. Everett loved every minute of the trip. The OT captain, Tony Monteuuis, surprised everyone by making a speech of thanks in French, and I amazed our host, Baron de Montesquieu, who was wearing his honorary OT cricket tie, by telling him that one of Napoleon's generals was an OT. In the mid-1980s Jack Davies followed Colin Cowdrey as President of the MCC; Christopher Cowdrey and Richard Ellison played cricket for England, while in the 1st XI, which lost very few matches but drew too many, Jonathan Longley broke F. H. Knott's long-standing record of 1,128 runs in a season. To cap it all the OT golfers won the Halford Hewitt in 1990. You just need to be patient. . . .

The frequent mention of cricket in these pages must infuriate both sport-haters and oarsmen. The Boat Club continues to occupy a large number of boys and masters. With the flow of water in the Medway so unpredictable and the better facilities available on nearby reservoirs, the top rowers carry on winter and summer unseen and unlauded. With the entry of a school VIII at Henley and good performances by the IVs at some of the less famous regattas, their achievements do not hit the headlines, but tribute must be paid to a long line of masters who have risked life and limb cycling along tow-paths in all winds and weathers. Some of them like Tom

Staveley, Philip Bathurst, Alfred Foster and Gifford Wood have had boats named after them. Others like Ted Bindloss and Nick Prosser have devoted similar effort to the Sailing Club.

In 1984 the new Hawden playing-fields were levelled and drains were installed. Their original name was Hawden, but it was felt they should be named after a famous OT. The name of E. M. Forster was suggested but rejected as inappropriate. He once told *The Tonbridgian* that the only thing he would write about was the abolition of compulsory sport. By coincidence *The Tonbridgian* in 1984 ran a poll on this subject. Sixty-eight per cent of the boys voted that they thought sport should be compulsory.

The same year a new sport was invented which the boys did not approve of – stonepicking. The new playing-fields had thrown up millions of stones, and no machine existed to pick them up. In 1838, when they levelled the Head, they used Irish navvies. In 1986 Everett decided to use boys and masters. There was a big row. Should it be done in lesson time or games time? It was decided to use both, which was surprising, since the new school rule on detention classes decreed that for bad work a boy should receive one hour's detention, but for cutting games he should receive two. The day of the great stonepicking was the coldest day of the century. They tried singing to keep up the boys' spirits, but, for many years to come, one generation of Tonbridgians will be able to tell their grandsons how tough life was at Tonbridge in their day.

In 1986 Everett was appointed chairman of the HMC – the first Headmaster of Tonbridge to be so honoured, and in 1988 was made a CBE. He never spared himself, travelling all over England and beyond to spread the name of the school. He helped the governors reorganize the

The Cricketer Cup party at Epernay, 1984. This picture, taken on a damp and cold day in October, outside the château, shows the whole party including wives, girl friends, the Headmaster, and the Baron de Montesquieu, wearing his OT cricket tie.

The winning Halford Hewitt Golf team – 1990.

David Kemp, acting Headmaster during 1990

Martin Hammond, formerly Headmaster of the City of London School, became Headmaster in September 1990.

school's funds so that more would be available for building. The sanatorium was sold, and a smaller sanatorium established next to the tuck-shop, more in keeping with modern medical needs and much nearer the playing-fields. The new building for School House was started, and Everett lived in hope of a magnificent new theatre and assembly hall.

He was instrumental in persuading the town council and the Sports Council to share the vast cost of renovating the running-track, so that the magnificent red Tartan track, which you can see when you are landing at Gatwick, now entertains about 40 schools a term for athletics matches, as well as being lent to the local clubs in the evenings and at week-ends. Colin Cowdrey, who frequently opens new cricket-net complexes with an exhibition of batting, could not be persuaded to do more than cut the tape when he officially opened the renovated running-track. Two new Astro turf pitches were completed, which should improve the standard of hockey, and Everett reluctantly agreed to the sale of the Fifty in the light of the probable building of a road across the New.

The pace of life must have been exhausting, but Everett's optimism saw him through. A serious fire in Ferox Hall and the hurricane of 1987 which destroyed many of the school's old trees brought out the best in him. In addition, in such a long headmastership, it was inevitable there should be some sad deaths and notable retirements. Three boys killed in road crashes in one holiday, boys dying of cancer, the sad news of the deaths of Robert Ogilvie and James McNeill – all must have affected him. The retirement of men of the calibre of Bill Werren, Clerk of Works for 46 years, and Ted Shellard, the Works Bursar, just two of many who had given the school so much, leaves holes almost impossible to fill. Some time ago Gilbert Hoole suggested the creation of a Book of Remembrance containing the names of all those who, since 1900, have served the school for a long time, and this was done in 1982. A very beautiful book can now be seen in the ante-chapel, and a page is turned every day.

Near the end of his time Christopher was beginning to look tired. He must have felt that he had achieved most of what he wanted. The school was in much better shape, and the fourth stage of the 40-year revival was near completion. Everything must have seemed nearly perfect, yet that was the moment for anxiety. Hubris and Nemesis are always with us.

On 17 September 1988, the chapel burnt down. At five past nine, just after the boys had left chapel to go to class, a wisp of smoke was seen coming from the roof. Three hours later there was nothing left except the walls. It was a disaster of such magnitude that words cannot describe it. Christopher Everett was magnificent. He rallied the boys, spoke on television and showed all his powers of leadership to get the school back to normal as quickly as possible. In effect we have gone full circle since Wolsey's question to the townsfolk in 1525. 'Would you like your old chapel back, or would you like a new one?' the Governors asked. To find the answer, you'll have to read the next school history.

In 1989 Everett accepted another position. His place was taken by David

The new School House. School House moved to its new buildings in November 1990.

Kemp, the loved and respected Second Master, who had done so much for Tonbridge for so long. One could even say of David Kemp that he is Tonbridge. In 1990 Martin Hammond, Headmaster of the City of London School, was appointed Headmaster. The Skinners' Company, who have fulfilled Sir Andrew Judde's wishes so well for so many centuries, have nearly always picked a winner. We hope he is as happy and successful here as his predecessors.

> When I'm a hundred, if I've been good,
> I'll go to Heaven and Sir Andrew Judde:
> I'll show my colours and he'll say to me
> 'Is the school the same as it used to be?'
>
> 'Well . . . No, Sir, not exactly.'

121

HEADMASTERS

Opposite top. *'Cricket on the Head', by Henry Wainwright, 1980. This oil painting of the Head on a summer evening, painted from the south-west corner, was specially commissioned from Henry Wainwright, a local artist. It shows the scene before the havoc wrought by the hurricane and the chapel fire.*

Opposite bottom. *The chapel burnt down on 17 September 1988.*

Revd. J. Proctor, MA	1553–1558
Revd. J. Lever, MA	1559–1574
Revd. J. Stockwood, MA	1574–1587
Revd. W. Hatch, MA	1587–1615
Revd. M. Jenkins, MA	1615–1624
Revd. J. Callis, MA	1624–1637
Revd. W. St J. Newman,. MA	1637–1640
T. Horne, MA	1640–1649
Revd. N. Gray, MA	1649–1660
Revd. J. Goad, BD	1660–1662
Revd. C. Wase, MA	1662–1668
Revd. T. Roots, MA	1668–1714
Revd. R. Spencer, MA	1714–1743
Revd. J. Cawthorn, MA	1743–1761
Revd. J. Towers, MA	1761–1772
Revd. V. Knox, BCL	1772–1778
Revd. V. Knox, MA, DD	1778–1812
Revd. T. Knox, MA, DD	1812–1843
Revd. J. I. Welldon, MA	1843–1875
Revd. T. B. Rowe, MA	1875–1890
Revd. J. Wood, MA, DD	1890–1898
Revd. C. C. Tancock, MA, DD	1898–1907
C. Lowry, MA	1907–1922
H. N. P. Sloman, MC, MA	1922–1939
E. E. A. Whitworth, MC, MA	1939–1949
Revd. L. H. Waddy, MA	1949–1962
M. McCrum, MA	1962–1970
R. M. Ogilvie, MA, D.Litt	1970–1975
C. H. D. Everett, MA	1975–1989
J. M. Hammond, MA	1990–

This aerial photo of the school shows the burnt-out chapel.

APPENDIX II

NUMBERS

Numbers before 1654 are not known, though they were probably about 50. From 1654 to 1721 a few lists survive; from 1721 on they are reasonably comprehensive. Until 1893 the numbers are for Skinners' Day; after that they are for 1 January.

1654 – 53	1784 – 85	1891 – 278	1942 – 306
1661 – 46	1794 – 26	1897 – 447	1945 – 405
1660 – 60	1813 – 44	1913 – 436	1948 – 465
1711 – 27	1843 – 83	1923 – 485	1960 – 524
1721 – 70	1845 – 139	1930 – 494	1970 – 580
1750 – 43	1860 – 182	1937 – 457	1980 – 670
1761 – 67	1870 – 214	1940 – 374	1990 – 632★
1774 – 17	1890 – 175		

★ In the last few years numbers have been reduced to allow for the new and smaller School House.

APPENDIX III

IMPORTANT DATES

1553 Original school building.

1631 Sundial on south end of Headmaster's house.

1663 East end of north gallery in parish church erected for use of the school.

1676 Hall or refectory.

1760 Skinners' school library (known as Cawthorn's Library).

1825 Cricket field bought.

1826 Lower School at north end of school.
New dining-hall. New dormitories upstairs.
House to north of school bought, later known as Old Judde.
Judde House started.
Dated iron-posts (scratching-posts) to mark limits of school property.

1827 Skinners' school library raised and enlarged. Outside altered to match new north end of school building.

1838 Head cricket ground levelled.

1845 Planting of Chestnut Avenue.

1849 Bat fives courts.

1851 C. Tattershall Dodd's picture of 'Cricket on the Head'.

1858 Three wooden classrooms at

side of playground.

1859 First school chapel.

1860 Cricket pavilion.

1863 Head cricket ground further levelled on north side.
Stone wall to north and brick wall to south of cricket ground.

1864 New school buildings.
Old buildings pulled down.

1866 Ferox Place bought and later pulled down. (Three cottages to south of school, opposite Ferox Hall.)

1867 Park House opened.

1873 Covered hand fives courts to south-east of Second cricket ground (Lower Hundred).
Second cricket ground levelled on west side.

1875 Hill Side opened.

1876 Corrugated-iron classroom for carpentry at side of playground.

1878 Parkside opened.

1879 Observatory.

1883 Land between High Street and the Avenue purchased.
Tonbridge School Mission in parish of Holy Cross founded.

1887 Science Building, including Physics and Chemistry laboratories, lecture room, drawing school, library, engine room, metal workshops, class-rooms.
Gymnasium.
Football ground in marshes hired until 1897.

1891 Cricket pavilion enlarged.

Tuck-shop.
Martin's field hired.

1892 Ferox Hall opened.
Temporary corrugated-iron chapel.
1859 chapel turned into a museum.
Three temporary iron class-rooms erected behind Science Building.

1893 Judde House moves to London Road.
Old Judde converted into sanatorium.
Day boys divided into Day boys 'A' and Day boys 'B'.
Bat fives courts removed (reputed to be only ones in the world).
Stagg's Land in Shipbourne Road hired.
Morris Tube range and armoury.

1894 Manor House opened.
New building erected between main building and Science Building, including Big School and clock tower, extra class-rooms, mechanical and biological laboratories, wood and metal workshops, housemaster's room, and cubicles for School House.
Wooden class-rooms on playground pulled down. Iron class-room moved to behind cricket pavilion.

1897 Swimming-bath in Hadlow Road.
Dale Memorial racket court.

Beeching's Land, Shipbourne Road (the Fifty) hired.

1900 Foundation stone of new chapel laid by Archbishop of Canterbury.

1902 Main part of new chapel consecrated.

1904 Beeching's Land and Stagg's Land purchased.

1907 Seven new fives courts next to Morris Tube range.
Two squash courts and an additional miniature range.
New tuck-shop.

1909 Completed chapel dedicated.

1910 New sanatorium in Shipbourne Road.
Parkside and Manor House purchased.

1914 Martin's Field and Potkiln Farm purchased.
Judde House purchased.

1915 New wood workshops erected.

1919 Ferox Hall and Bordyke cottages purchased.

1922 Temporary class-rooms in Dry Hill House garden.

1923 Park House and Hill Side purchased.
Walter Pattisson football pavilion on the Fifty.

1925 War memorial dedicated.

1926 Dry Hill House acquired for day boys.

1927 New Music School.
Library moves to Old Big School.

1932 New tuckshop. Old tuckshop becomes school shop.

1932 Day boys 'A' and Day boys 'B' renamed Welldon House and Smythe House respectively.

1933 School Mission renamed Tonbridge Club in St Pancras. New Club building in St Pancras opened by Lord Mayor.

1935 New squash courts.

1936 New Biology Laboratory and Art School opened by Duke of Kent.

1938 Library moves to Old Chapel.

1952 Knox House opened.

1953 Quatercentenary – wall in front of school.
Visit by Queen Elizabeth, the Queen Mother.

1958 Chestnut Avenue cut down.

1962 Smythe Library, South Wing House, and Ironside cloister opened by Princess Alexandra.

1967 First Senior Student house opened.

1968 Climbing wall.

1969 Potkiln Farm site levelled.

1970 H. S. Vere Hodge bequeaths High Trees to the Skinners' Company.

1971 Wilmot running-track and hard hockey pitch.

1973 New Biology Laboratory.

1974 Whitworth House opened and Knox House closed.

1975 New swimming-bath opened.

1978 New Technology Department.

1983 Hawden playing-fields purchased and Baths fields sold.

1984	Welldon House moves to Leelands.	1990	New School House opens next to Greywalls.
1985	Running-track renovated and improved.		Governors decide to renovate and extend chapel (projected re-opening – 1993).
1988	Chapel burnt down.		
1989	Temporary chapel on Quad. New all-weather hockey pitch.	1991	Sale of the Fifty, the New, the Elms and Yardley Court playing-fields completed.
	New 1st XV pitch levelled on Le Flemings.		OTs win Cricketer Cup for 6th time

The inter-house singing competition, or 'House Shout' as it was affectionately called started in the late nineteenth century but was finally a victim of the changes of the 1960s. It used to consist of two parts, a song sung by almost the whole house (one or two growlers could be omitted) and a song by a small choir. Some very eminent musicians came to the school to judge it in their time.

Chris Reid, already a promising poet at school, who went on to win the Somerset Maugham Award and the Hawthornden Prize, was also a talented cartoonist.

IMPRESSION OF A HOUSE SHOUT

APPENDIX IV

The following statistics have been collected by Andrew Zaltzman of Smythe House. As he had to work in his limited free time and with limited access to *Wisden* and *The Tonbridgian*, he may have missed someone out or made a few errors. His introduction to the subject at the age of 16 has given him the urge to write a more detailed book on Tonbridge cricket later. Meanwhile for more detailed research on cricket up to 1947, please consult P. J. R. Bathurst's splendid articles in *The Tonbridgian*.

Test cricketers – 6: J. C. Hartley, K. L. Hutchings, M. C. Cowdrey, R. M. Prideaux, R. M. Ellison, C. S. Cowdrey.

Rugger internationals – 21

County cricketers – 43 (at least)

SCHOOL CRICKET RESULTS (1856–1990)

	P.	W.	L.	
★Dulwich	93	39	23	1874–1911; 1931–90
★Lancing	76	46	9	1878–94; 1918–40; 1945–90
★Clifton	73	28	16	1899–90; 1915–90
Brighton	69	24	28	1856–94
★Haileybury	52	17	15	1915–19; 1941–90
★Bedford	46	15	8	1941–43; 1947–90
Christ's Hosp.	38	22	7	1942–81
Westminster	31	22	3	1915–20; 1927; 1952–79
Sherborne	26	12	2	1905–15; 1925–40
★Eastbourne	22	9	3	1940; 1969–90
★Felsted	21	7	6	1969–90
★Winchester	19	8	3	1970–90
★Wellington	19	8	4	1971–90
★Charterhouse	14	4	5	1942–45; 1981–90
Sevenoaks	14	6	0	1975–89
★Eton	4	0	1	1987–90
★Harrow	3	0	1	1988–90
All schools	675	299	157	

★ = current fixtures

SCHOOL RUGGER RESULTS (1870–1990)

	P.	W.	L.	
★Dulwich	101	42	48	1874–1911; 1932–90
★Haileybury	90	34	45	1891–92; 1900–90
★Uppingham	72	22	48	1911–38; 1946–90
★Harrow	61	28	29	1928–90
★Christ's Hosp.	50	25	23	1939–90
★Eastbourne	50	26	19	1939–90
★Sherborne	39	19	15	1895–1915; 1919–38
★Wellington	33	8	22	1914–15; 1960–90
★King's Cant.	31	16	13	1959–90
★Judd	24	12	12	1968–90
★Sevenoaks	23	9	11	1967–90
All schools	643	272	315	

★ = current fixtures

CRICKET

BEST BATTING TOTALS IN A SEASON

		Innings	Not Out	Highest	Total	Average	100s	50s
1986	J. I. Longley	18	1	156★	1141	67.12	4	5
1910	F. H. Knott	14	0	187	1126	80.43	6	4
1919	L. P. Hedges	13	1	193	1038	86.50	4	3
1950	M. C. Cowdrey	15	2	175★	1033	79.46	4	5
1987	J. I. Longley	18	1	129	1007	59.24	3	7
1975	C. S. Cowdrey	18	6	122★	966	80.50	3	7
1921	H. C. A. Gaunt	16	2	198★	960	68.57	4	3
1965	D. R. Aers	16	3	130★	914	70.31	2	7
1921	T. E. S. Francis	16	3	173★	886	68.15	4	3
1978	J. C. Spurling	17	4	135★	866	66.62	3	5

OVER 50 WICKETS IN A SEASON

	Wickets	Average		Wickets	Average
1939 M. P. Rose-Price	78	11.35	1877 G. F. D. Hamilton	52	8.3
1908 C. Marzetti	63	13.04	1888 L. L. Reid	52	8.5
1926 E. J. G. Tucker	63	13.7	1887 C. J. Kortright	52	11.35
1887 L. L. Reid	60	9.1	1937 P. R. Stevens	52	16.69
1938 D. G. W. Yeats-Brown	59	15.39	1937 B. N. S. Kidson	51	17.16
1940 R. A. A. Smith	58	10.54	1932 R. W. M. Morrison	50	12.94
1908 H. M. Bannister	57	12.40	1953 R. M. K. Gracey	50	14.70
1888 C. J. Kortright	53	7.2			

POSTSCRIPT

As this is a pictorial history of the school, I have had to restrict the number of words I could write in each section. Many facts I would like to have included have had to be omitted. I have had to limit my inclusion of individual names and apologize to those I have offended, either by mentioning them or by not doing so. My biggest problem has been when and where to use capital letters. This is very much a personal account. I started as a novi in Judde House in 1944 and finished as master in charge of Clare House right opposite Judde House in 1987. 50 yards in 43 years. Sir Sidney Smith and H. C. Stewart make me feel very inadequate. I could have dedicated this book to many people, especially my mentor Gilbert Hoole, to Lawrence Waddy, who has shown me so much kindness, to my long-suffering friends the Batterbys, to my old colleagues, especially Mike Bushby, David Kemp, Ted Shellard and Bill Werren, or to my Aunt Ruby, whose dining-table I ruined by turning Welldon's 'Yearbook' round on it a hundred times. I decided, finally, to dedicate it to my brother, who first filled my head with stories of Tonbridge, when I was seven years old.

H.B.O.

1991

INDEX

129

© Tonbridge School   First published 1991   ISBN 0 907383 25 4
Published by James & James (Publishers) Limited
75 Carleton Road, London N7 0ET
Typeset by Columns of Reading and Printed in Great Britain by
The Hollen Street Press at Slough, Berkshire
Bound by Hunter & Foulis Limited, Edinburgh